12/2013

Mary

[signature]

Santa & Sam

by

Larry Bielat & Debra Rousso

With

Chris Warner

Cover Design & Layout by Jamie Welch (www.jamie-welch.com)
Snowflake Art By Emma Claire Warner

© Copyright 2012 *Wagon Publishing*
ISBN# 978-0-9884880-0-7
Fairhope, Alabama

Introduction

World-renowned, Santa Claus is a combination of folk legends and myths that have developed over centuries, and across cultures. The forerunner for Santa Claus is Bishop Nicholas, of Smyrna, which today is Turkey.

Nicholas lived in the 4th century A.D. He was wealthy, generous and loved children. Often he delivered happiness to poor children by placing gifts unannounced on their windowsills as they slept on Christmas Eve. The church later lifted Nicholas to a position of great esteem. St. Nicholas became the Patron Saint of Children and Seafarers.

In America the legend of "Santa Claus" traces its origins to the Dutch yarn of "Sinter Klaas," brought to New York by Dutch settlers during the 17th century.

Washington Irving's "History of New York" in 1809, described the arrival of "Saint Nicholas" on horseback on Christmas Eve. After the Civil War, Santa Claus was widely depicted in American newspapers.

Today, Santa Claus's universal appeal is as broad as his bellowing midriff…the ageless, timeless, immortal white-bearded, cherub-like man who bears gifts for all at Christmas.

Chapter One

December 12
Madison, Wisconsin

Sam Adams whistled "Jingle Bells" as he pulled the front door shut and with a click turned the key in the lock. A muted meow called his attention to the picture window. Badger, head poking through the lacey curtains, gazed at Sam with unblinking eyes.

"Don't worry old fellow. I'll be back before you know it," he reassured the cat.

Sam turned to walk down the porch steps when the vestibule phone rang. His shoulders dropped in exasperation. He fumbled for his keys and re-opened the door. He trudged through the threshold and with misty breath answered the phone.

"Hello!"

"I didn't wake you, did I?" the familiar voice on the line asked.

Sam grimaced and stared up at his majestic, ticking grandfather clock. It was almost 10 a.m.

"It's 10 o'clock! I wasn't sleeping!"

"Well, the last time I called—it was four in the afternoon—and you were sleeping!"

"That was a nap!" Sam defended.

"Oh. That was a nap, huh?"

"What do you want, Leo?"

"It's Tuesday! We're supposed to get together tonight, like always, and I wanted to make sure you were still coming over. Are you gonna make it like we planned?"

The Tiger cat emerged from behind the curtains and stared up at Sam.

"Is it Tuesday?"

"Yes it's Tuesday! And you wonder why I have to call!"

"Okay, okay. I just forgot. I'll see you around five, like always."

"Alright, bye," Leo said. He abruptly hung up the phone.

Sam wheezed loudly and looked at the receiver. He returned it to its cradle. He smiled, shook his head and continued whistling. He again crossed the threshold and locked the door. As he turned to navigate the porch steps, he noticed it felt like snow was in the air. Dank, bone-chilling fingers of cold tickled Sam's neck. Tugging the collar of his tweed mackinaw, he carefully descended the stairs, 75-year old knees creaking in protest.

The walk to the corner grocery seemed to get longer every trip. Sam could have driven his car, but he was afraid that if he stopped walking to the store he would stop altogether. He hated being afraid, but ever since Irene died a year earlier, he was afraid of everything—afraid of falling, afraid of dying, afraid of living.

His doctor's dire predictions about his failing heart only fueled his fears.

"Sam, you need to slow down, take better care of yourself," his doctor again warned a month earlier. "If you don't slow down and remember to take your medication, you might not see next Christmas. Why not consider selling your home and moving into an assisted living facility?"

Assisted living facility, indeed! To Sam, what the doctor really meant was death's waiting room—pitiful old people slumped in wheel chairs just waiting their turn.

"No thanks," Sam thought as he started up Dunbar Street. "When I go I'm going to die right in my own home."

Sam had lived on the oak tree lined Dunbar Street in Madison, Wisconsin for nearly fifty years. When he and Irene were first married they rented a small apartment in one of the larger houses near Main Street across from the campus until they saved enough for a down payment on a house of their own. They enjoyed 47 years of happy living in the cozy two-story brick home. Now, Sam rattled about the house, lonely and heart-broken.

But as of 9:30 a.m. that morning, things were looking better. Roger had called. It was definite—his son and family were coming home to Madison for Christmas. Sam had been waiting for the news for more than two weeks. Roger's job was demanding and more often than not, it was impossible for him to get away during the holidays.

Ah yes, things were looking better. Even the overcast sky didn't put a damper on Sam's good spirits. Roger was coming home.

Sam made his way down the sidewalk. He passed hurriedly in front of St. Ambrose's Catholic Church and School, a building with a classic dark brick steeple. Bundled children played outside at recess. He noticed Father Vince, a portly, silver-haired Italian priest, coming out the front door of the rectory.

"Sam Adams? I haven't seen you at seven o'clock mass. You used to be a weekly regular. Are things okay?"

Sam looked embarrassed. He looked away.

"Hi Father. I've been okay. It's just...I'm fine. It's just I don't have much motivation now that Irene is gone. It's tough on me, so many memories, you know?"

Sam hung his head.

"Sam, I understand completely. You and Irene were as close and active as a couple can be. The Altar Society misses her almost as much as you do, I can assure you."

Father Vince placed his right hand on Sam's left shoulder.

"Come to mass this Sunday, Sam. Saint Ambrose misses you and we'd love to have you back...I'm sure the Lord would too."

Sam looked up to Father Vince.

"Sounds like a good idea Father. I'll try and make it."

Father Vince looked into Sam's heavy eyes.

"God bless you, Sam. Remember we're always here for you."

He paused.

"It was great seeing you Sam! I'll see you at mass! Merry Christmas!

"Good seeing you, Father. Merry Christmas to you too."

Sam shook Father Vince's hand, pulled his collar to his neck and continued his walk. The wind and snow flurries grew heavier. Sam shivered and quickened his deliberate pace. Moments later, two houses down from the church, Sam was startled by a shrill call.

"Sam. Sam." Evelyn Baldwin's voice, which was in Sam's opinion, about two octaves too high, shattered Sam's thoughts.

"Evelyn, you're looking quite lovely this morning," Sam said to Evelyn from her covered wooden porch.

"A warm ray of sunshine on a cold and dreary day." Sixty-eight- year-old Evelyn blushed like a schoolgirl right to the roots of her somewhat purplish hair.

"Sam, you old tease. Are you sure you won't come to supper tomorrow?" she pleaded. Her voice made Sam wince ever so slightly.

"Ah, Evelyn. Thank you for the invitation, but I have a lot of work to do. Roger and his family are coming for Christmas. He just called this morning and said they were definitely coming. He arranged things so that he could take a week off from work."

"That's wonderful!" Evelyn thrilled. "It's about time they came to visit! What with knowing how alone you are without Irene. How old are those adorable grandchildren of yours?"

The wind blew the snow harder, swirling around Sam's head. He pulled his collar to him. Snowflakes fell from his head down the back of his neck.

"They're growing up so fast, Evelyn. Christopher is 14, and can you believe it, my beautiful little Jenna is 10 years old already? I don't know where the time goes."

"We're all getting old, Sam. I'll tell you, I feel it more and more every day."

Sam's ears had about reached their tolerance level and he tried to find a graceful way to say goodbye. But Evelyn was not done; she had a bit of gossip she needed to share.

"Did you hear about Sadie Cohen?"

Before he could reply, Evelyn took a deep breath and chirped on.

"Her house was broken into last week while she was at her synagogue, in broad daylight, none-the-less. They took her mother's wedding ring and her television set, the poor old dear. Mrs. Hopewell says Sadie is so afraid that she wants to put in a security system. I don't know how she will ever afford it. That no-good rascal Ben she was married to hardly left her a dime. I'll bet she doesn't even have the money to replace the television, let alone buy a security system. I'll tell you…"

"Well, what a shame," Sam commiserated, glancing over his shoulder to look back at his own home. He was glad he had remembered to lock his door this time. "Things are changing. Twenty years ago we never locked our doors. Well, I need to run now, Evelyn. I've got a job to do with Roger coming home."

Sam breathed a visible sigh of relief as he made his escape from Evelyn's well-meaning chatter.

"What a shame about Sadie. I hope someone does something for her," he thought. "I better get moving," he muttered, futilely searching his coat pockets for his gloves. "My joints will freeze up before I get to the store."

Sam briskly rubbed his cold hands together and jammed them deep into his coat pockets. He mentally chastised himself for forgetting his gloves again. Standing still for so long listening to Evelyn had made him quite chilly.

Sam continued up Dunbar, mentally reviewing his "things-to-do-before-Roger-gets-here" list. Just like the walk to the store, the list seemed to keep getting longer and longer. "Buy a Christmas tree; get the decorations down from the attic; make sure the bedding is clean; buy presents; wrap presents; bake cookies."

"I've less than two weeks to get all this done," he anxiously thought. "I can't be wasting time chitchatting with the neighbors. Roger is coming home."

Sam was suddenly startled.

"Ching-ching, ching-ching."

"Mr. Adams, Mr. Adams. Watch out, here I come!"

Sam turned to look over his shoulder. Six-year-old Jason Wendell, an African-American, was quickly closing in. His bell rang loudly and his legs furiously pumped the tricycle pedals. Sam stepped off the sidewalk to safety just as Jason came to a toe-dragging stop.

"My, young fellow, you were going so fast you were almost flying!" Sam said with a smile.

"That was nuttin'!'," Jason bragged with a gap-toothed grin. "Wait till you see how fast I'm gonna go on my new super-charged bike!"

"You're getting a new bike?"

"Sure am. It's gonna be red, with just two wheels. No more baby-bike for me! I been real good and I'm gonna get it from Santa!"

Sam looked at the rusty, battered old tricycle upon which Jason was perched. He knew that last year Jason's father had abandoned his wife and young son and that Jason's mother was struggling to make ends meet. He seriously doubted she had the extra money to buy Jason a new bike.

"Jason, you know this bike you have here still looks to have some miles left on it. Maybe you can ride it for another year," Sam gently proposed.

"No way! I'm done with this baby bike! I know I'm getting a new bike for Christmas. I saw Santa at the community center and he said if I was a very good boy I would get my wish. I wrote him a letter, too, in case he forgot he saw me."

Sam looked down at Jason's earnest face and knew there would be a really disappointed little boy on Christmas morning.

"You know, Jason, Santa is busy this time of year."

"He won't forget," Jason confidently replied.

"I hope not Jason. I hope not."

"Where you going Mr. Adams?"

"I'm going to the grocery. And I've got to hurry. I have a lot to do. My son and grandchildren are coming to visit me for Christmas."

"Okay. See ya Mr. Adams." Jason turned his tricycle around and headed home, rusted wheels shrieking loudly.

"Poor kid," Sam thought. "I sure hope someone does something for Jason and his mom."

Sam proceeded with his walk, stepping his pace up a bit to make up for lost time. His breath came in rapid puffs of white steam. By the time he arrived at the grocery store he needed to sit on the bench outside the electric glass doors.

"You okay there, Mr. Adams?" asked Barbara, a working-class, forty-something woman, who had just finished a smoke break.

"Whew, just catching my breath. I'll be okay Barbara."

"You sure?"

"I guess that quack Dr. Hudson might be right. He's been telling me to take it easy, but well, you know how it is." Sam opened his small black pillbox with cold-stiffened fingers and tried to remove one of two small tablets.

"Here, let me do that for you," Barbara said as she took one out and handed it to him.

"Thanks," said Sam. He slipped the pill underneath his tongue. "I'll be alright in just a second."

Barbara Donovan, the store's head cashier, watched Sam with a cautious eye. Soon Sam's breathing slowed and his color improved.

"Do you want me to call a cab for you Mr. Adams?" she asked.

"No, heavens no. I'm okay now. I was just walking a little too fast. I need to pick up a couple of things for Badger and me for dinner." Sam breathed easier now.

"Okay, but let me know if you need help."

"I will. Thank you again."

Barbara started to stand. Sam stopped her with a hand on her arm.

"Barbara, how's your husband doing?"

She paused and half smiled. She checked her watch and nervously pulled the crumpled cigarette pack from the pocket of her khaki pants. In one fluid motion she adroitly flicked one from the package and lit it with her handy disposable lighter.

"As well can be expected, I guess. Bob's been out of work so long and his medical insurance isn't covering as much as we hoped it would, especially the physical therapy, but we'll squeak by like we always do. Won't be much of a Christmas this year, but the kids are older and they understand. Would you believe that they told us not to buy a Christmas tree this year? They tried to convince me a tree wasn't important."

"They're good kids, Barbara. They know how hard you work," Sam said.

"I was hoping to scrape enough together for a small tree. It won't seem much like the holidays without a tree in the house, but the trees are so expensive. It does seem like a waste of money. Maybe the kids are right," Barbara sighed.

"Of course they are," Sam agreed. "You're all together. That's what's really important. Did I tell you Roger and his family are coming for Christmas? I have so much to do to get ready. I guess I never realized how hard Irene worked to make the holidays so perfect."

"That's wonderful Mr. Adams! I'm glad they're coming to be with you. Are you sure you're feeling okay? I've got to get back to work; my break is almost over. Let me walk you inside."

"Yes, yes. I'm fine Barbara. Thank you."

"What a shame," Sam mused as he pushed his shopping cart down the grocery aisle. "I sure hope someone does something for them or they're going to have one miserable holiday."

Leaning heavily on the cart, Sam made his way through the store, selecting a few things here and there. Counting the groceries in his cart Sam was dismayed to see that he had nine items, one more than the express checkout allowed. Looking at the winding line of full shopping carts waiting to be tallied, Sam decided he really didn't need that jar of peanuts. After returning the nuts to their proper shelf, he took his rightful place in the express line.

"Mr. Sam! Mr. Sam!" Boomed a familiar voice.

Sam looked around the two people standing in front of him to see Doug the grocery bagger grinning broadly and vigorously waving his hand.

"How are you today, Mr. Sam? Merry Christmas! How are you today?" Doug bellowed.

A frown from the cashier brought Doug's attention back to his task at hand. Using great care, he bagged the items as they came down the conveyor belt.

Doug was an energetic young man in his late twenties who lived in a group home with four other handicapped adults. He took his position as a bagger quite seriously and was a talkative yet dependable employee. Mr. Sam, who always took time to talk to Doug, was his most favorite customer. Finally, it was Sam's turn to check out. Doug couldn't wait to tell him the good news.

"Mr. Sam, Mr. Sam, did you know that Christmas is just three days away?"

"No, Doug. Christmas is thirteen days from today," Sam gently corrected.

"Thirteen days? That's a lot more than three days isn't it?" Times and dates were concepts that Doug had not completely been able to master.

"It's ten more days, but that's not too many more. Christmas will be here before you know it."

Doug carefully placed Sam's purchases in a paper bag making sure to put the bread on top so it wouldn't be crushed.

"Mr. Sam, Santa is bringing me a pet for Christmas."

"Is he now?" Sam countered doubtfully. "Where would Doug get the idea that Santa was going to bring him a pet?" Sam wondered.

"Yes he is. He told me himself," Doug replied with confidence. "I saw Santa at the community center and he told me that if I was good he would bring me a pet of my own."

Sam frowned as he recalled that Jason also had been promised a seemingly impossible gift by the community center Santa. "You know, Doug, Santa is really busy this time of year. Maybe you misunderstood him?"

"Oh, no Mr. Sam! He said he will bring me a pet. Did you know Christmas is only six days away?"

"Christmas will be here soon, Doug. Thanks for bagging my groceries. You did a great job." Sam placed a quarter in Doug's hand.

"Merry Christmas Mr. Sam! Thank you. Maybe I will name my pet Mr. Sam!" Doug laughed at his own joke in big guffawing chuckles.

"Merry Christmas Doug."

Sam picked up his grocery bag and began the long walk home. "I sure hope somebody comes through on Christmas for Doug, or he will be very disappointed," he thought, shaking his head in wonderment at Doug's steadfast belief in Santa.

The day had grown colder. The snow fell thicker. Sam was even sorrier that he had forgotten his gloves. But in spite of the frigidness, Sam was happier than he had been in a long time.

This Christmas was going to be a special one. Sam just knew it. He had always held the magic of Christmas close to his heart. Since his youth Sam anticipated and loved the holiday season. But after Irene passed away, the seasonal joy abandoned him.

Sam spent the last Christmas at Roger's home in California, but it wasn't the same. First, it was too warm; and they had an artificial tree. Roger's wife didn't like real trees because they shed needles on her white carpet. And, they went out for Christmas dinner —to a Chinese restaurant of all places. No, no, that wasn't Christmas at all. But Sam knew this year it would be different, because Roger and his children were coming *home*.

Chapter Two

December 16
11:00 a.m.

"That's the last of em' Badger. Who would have thought things could get this dirty in just a couple of years," Sam grumbled as he mopped his sweaty face with a not-so-white handkerchief. Badger sniffed the dusty boxes and sneezed in feline agreement.

Sam wearily surveyed the pile of cartons of Christmas decorations that he had spent most of the morning lugging down from the attic.

"Well, we better get to work, Badger. These boxes aren't going to unpack themselves." But Badger had other ideas about how to spend the remainder of the afternoon. The over-sized Tiger cat leapt nimbly onto the sofa and promptly settled down for a nap.

"Good-for-nothing freeloader!" Sam affectionately muttered.

Sam's joints creaked loudly as he knelt down beside the carton heap. Taking a deep breath, he opened the first of the boxes and lifted out a tissue-wrapped object. With trembling hands he carefully removed the paper to reveal of all things a snowflake made from Popsicle sticks.

"Dad, Dad! Look what we made in school today!"

Sam looked up from grading his students' final exams, as 8-year old Roger burst into the den.

"What have you got son?"

"A snowflake, Dad. We ate popsicles and made snowflakes out of the Popsicle sticks!"

Sam reverently took the wooden snowflake from Roger's chubby fist. To Sam's eyes the crooked, glue-gobbed and glitter-dusted snowflake was a work of art.

"It's perfect Roger. It's just what our tree needs. Let's go show Mom!"

Roughly rubbing the back of his hand across his eyes, Sam sat back on his heels and whispered, "How can such a wonderful memory hurt so much, Irene?" Sam didn't expect an answer, of course, but since her death he couldn't seem to shake the habit of talking to her. He felt her presence so strongly that often he had to look twice to convince himself that she wasn't in the room.

Irene was the love of Sam's life. Not a single day of their more than 50-year marriage passed without Sam marveling over the fact that Irene loved him. From the moment he first saw her at the University of Wisconsin's freshman Christmas party he knew he was in love.

Sam huddled inside the gymnasium with a group of buddies who also had arrived stag at the freshman mixer. They were discussing the football team's prospects for the next season when they were interrupted by a cheerful "Ho, ho, ho!"

A quite authentic looking Santa slapped Sam on the back and again gave a hearty "ho, ho, ho!"

"Merry Christmas young fellows! What can Santa bring you for Christmas this year?" the jolly old soul asked Sam.

"Thanks for asking Santa," Sam said. "What I could really use for Christmas this year is an 'A' in economics." Sam smiled infectiously and winked at his friends. "What do you think, Santa? Can your elves handle that?"

"Is that all? Well let's see; I don't know about an 'A,' but how about a tutor? I understand that young lady over there is quite a whiz in economics," Santa said as he pointed across the room.

Sam turned to see whom Santa chose. The economic whiz was a vision of what you would imagine the sugar plum fairy might look like. Dressed in the softest of pink, with golden blonde hair tumbling around her shoulders and eyes as blue as a June sky, Irene was the most wondrously beautiful woman Sam had ever seen.

Sam had no phony notions about his own good looks, or rather, his lack of them. He knew he was as tall and skinny as a beanpole, with a hound dog sort of face. But he had a quick wit and a good humor about him and a very kind soul—at least that's what Irene told him in later years. But right then, he knew his heart would stop beating if he didn't hear her voice.

Sam desperately looked to Santa for help but all he got was a wink and a grin. So, he took a fortifying gulp of eggnog, straightened his bow tie, and pulled at the too-short sleeves of his borrowed sports coat. Drawing a deep breath and silently praying that he wouldn't trip over his own feet, he crossed the room.

Standing in front of her with knees shaking so hard that he was sure she could hear them rattle, he tried desperately to think of something witty and sophisticated to say—something that would make her fall instantly in love with him. But once he looked into her lovely face all he could manage was a strangled, "Hello, I'm, er, um, Sam."

Irene's clear blue eyes warmed with a smile. In the background Sam could hear her friends giggling quietly. "Oh now I've done it," he thought. "Her friends think it's so funny that I am even trying to talk to her that they can't stop laughing."

Sam murmured a sad apology for intruding and started to walk away. Irene stopped him with a gentle touch of her hand on his coat sleeve. He turned toward her, but Irene was not looking at him; she was looking up at the basketball rim. As he followed her gaze upward, Sam realized that they were standing beneath mistletoe. He felt the blush start at his toes and rapidly burn its way to the tip top of his head.

Without a sound, Irene stood on her tiptoes and lightly brushed her lips against his cheek. "Merry Christmas, Sam, my name is Irene." she whispered. Sam felt his heart race and his blood roar. He knew he would love her forever.

Sam still vividly remembered every moment of that wonderful evening—the way Irene felt in his arms as they danced; the way the moonlight shimmered on the snow as they walked to her dorm; and the way his heart soared when they shared their first, fumbling kiss good night.

From that moment Sam and Irene were inseparable. They married exactly one year later, on the 23rd of December, and Irene fittingly carried a tiny sprig of mistletoe in her bouquet. Christmas became their special passion. It was always a time of love and joy, a time of hope and happiness.

Irene stopped attending classes soon after they were married, a decision she never regretted. She got a job in the campus bookstore. She was thrilled to be Sam's wife and they planned on starting a family when Sam graduated.

The years rolled on. Sam finished his undergraduate and graduate degrees, with no small measure of help from his special tutor, and became a humanities professor at his alma mater. They bought a house and went about making it a home. But the babies didn't come. For years they hoped to have a child and time and time again they faced disappointment.

As Christmases passed without a family of their own, Sam and Irene immersed themselves in the spirit of the holiday. They gave their time and love to others. They visited children in the hospital as well as patients in nursing homes. Furthermore, they always found time to help the church take care of needy Madison families.

Sam donned the bright red Santa suit that Irene made. They laughed themselves silly as they annually stuffed pillows into the suit and glued the fake white beard to his chin. But every Christmas Sam would look into Irene's lovely face and see the pain she hid in her heart. The one gift she wanted so badly—a child—he had not been able to give her. Twice she became pregnant only to miscarry. The buildup and letdown was torturous for both of them, but especially for Irene.

Then, everything changed. One Christmas, 14 years after they were married, Irene was pregnant. They were overcome with joy. When they had given up any hope of ever becoming parents, a miracle happened. In late summer of the next year, Roger Samuel Adams was born a squealing, wrinkle-faced bundle of love and happiness.

Chapter Three

From a seated position in his favorite chair Sam examined the mountain of Christmas chaos on display in his living room. The many boxes remained where he set them. He realized they weren't going to unpack themselves. He shook his head in an attempt to clear his thoughts.

"Where did the time go?" he fretted. "I'm never going to be ready when Roger gets here."

"Ring."

"Ring."

The persistent jingle of the telephone jolted Sam from his thoughts. He grimaced as he stood, muscles stiff.

"Ring."

"Ring."

"I'm coming. Hold your horses!

"Hello."

"Sam! It's me, Leo. Where in the hell are you? I called you this morning, remember? What are you doing over there—nappin' again? You're late!"

Sam said nothing. He glanced out the window. To his surprise, the streetlights flickered to life. He checked his watch. It was 5:10 p.m., almost dinnertime. He had forgotten about Leo.

"Sam? Are you okay?" Leo intently asked.

"Yeah, Leo. I'm fine. Just a little tired. I apologize. I must have lost track of time. I'll be there in, let's see, how's half an hour sound? Can you wait that long you old goat?"

"I'll try, but hurry up!"

Sam hung up the phone. He felt bad for not remembering his friend. It's just that he was so busy.

"I'm never going to be ready when Roger gets here. I'll have to work harder tomorrow," he thought.

As Sam shrugged into his woolen overcoat, a mutinous meow and a not-too-gentle bump on the shins reminded him of another obligation.

"Badger, sorry old fellow, I almost forgot you too. I don't know what's going on today. Well, let's get you fed. Leo can just wait another couple of minutes."

Sam walked to the kitchen with Badger close on his heels.

"What will it be today, old boy? Tuna?"

Badger meowed his approval.

"Enjoy your dinner. I'll tell Leo you said hello," Sam chuckled.

Sam turned to leave, but a nagging thought that he was forgetting something popped into his head. He wondered what it was.

"Your medicine, Sam!" Irene's voice rang clear and true as if she was in the kitchen with him, but Sam knew that her voice was just in his heart.

Sam opened the cabinet and took out a bottle of medication. He was supposed to take a tablet three times a day, but more often than not he forgot. Sometimes Irene would remind him, although lately it seemed she too forgot.

Downing the pill without the benefit of water caused it to stick to his throat. Sam swallowed hard and the pill finally made its way down.

"Getting old is rough, Badger. But I guess you know that too, don't you? We've been together for a long time old fellow…"

It was their first Christmas without their son. Roger was vacationing with his wife's family in the Colorado Rockies.

Sam and Irene missed Roger, their daughter-in-law and their three-year-old grandson Christopher, but still they held on to holiday traditions. Irene baked batches of cookies and made rag dolls for the children spending Christmas in the hospital. Sam wrapped the presents that the faculty members donated.

It was a long day. Sam and Irene weren't as young as they had once been, but they still made their Christmas Eve rounds. By the end of the evening their spirits were lifted and their joy restored.

Sam took Irene home, but he still had one more stop to make.

"I'll be back in a little while, Irene. It's cold out here and this Santa suit is a lot warmer than your outfit."

"I'll brew up a nice hot cup of Irish coffee," Irene promised. "Hurry back!"

Sam watched her climb the steps to the front porch, his heart filled with love.

Sam's last visit of the evening was to the Miller house. Mrs. Miller's husband had passed away two years prior and the young widow was desperately trying to make a happy Christmas for her three small children. Money was scarce and Sam knew she couldn't afford much in the way of presents.

But Sam was going to come through once again. Tucked in the trunk of his car were gaily-wrapped presents that he had coaxed local merchants into donating.

Sam's car rolled slowly to a stop in front of the Miller home just as a new snowfall began to swirl. With black boots crunching on the already snow-covered front steps, Sam lugged the full box of presents up the stairs and set it down at the front door.

Sam walked back to his car and leaned against the fender absently rubbing at the dull ache in his chest. Sometimes being Santa was strenuous work.

As he stood there, Sam became aware of the sound of someone whistling "Jingle Bells."

When he looked down the street he saw a Santa Claus strolling toward him. This was one of those well-dressed, department store-type Santas; but instead of a full sack slung over his shoulder, this Santa carried a small carton.

"Hello Santa," Sam called.

"Hello to you," the dapper Santa replied. "Working late too, I see."

"Well, I'm done now. This was my last delivery and so it's back home to Mrs. Claus," Sam joked.

"Maybe you can do me a favor," the Santa said. "I've made all of my deliveries in Madison, but I still have this one box left. Do you think you could find someone to give it to?"

"I can always find someone in need of a Christmas gift," Sam answered.

"Here you go then," the Santa said as he handed Sam the carton.

"Merry Christmas, Sam."

Sam looked down at the carton in his hands. "Thank you," he started to say. His head snapped up.

"Hey, wait a minute! How did you know my name?" Sam stammered. He looked all around. But no one was there. The street was as deserted as it had been a minute earlier. Sam blinked his eyes and peered through the quickly falling snow.

A soft meowing sound brought his attention back to the carton in his hands. Cautiously he lifted the lid. Inside two bright eyes gazed up at him. The tiny kitty meowed louder.

"Hey there little fellow. So you are a leftover Christmas present…Who can I give you to at this late hour?" he mused as he tickled the kitten's furry chin.

Sam shuddered as a cold wind whipped the snow around them. He suddenly remembered Irene's promise of hot coffee.

"Let's go home, kitty. I'll decide what to do with you later."

Sam entered the car and started the motor.

"The heat will come on in just a minute," he said. The shivering kitty didn't look convinced. Sam noticed.

"What have I got in here that will warm you up?" Sam said aloud as he reached over the seat and rummaged in the back of the car. "Here you go— this old Wisconsin badger's sweatshirt should do the trick."

"Seems I still haven't decided what to do with you Badger," Sam said as he smiled fondly at the old cat. Badger was going about his usual after-dinner grooming and really didn't take much notice of Sam. Sam looked at his watch and silently shrieked.

"I'd better get going or Leo's going to have my head. Speaking of head, where did I leave my hat this time?" Sam wondered. "Oh well, I'll be back in a couple of hours. Leave the Christmas decorations alone Badger."

Before leaving Sam filled a small medicine bottle with triple malt scotch and took a cigar from the humidor on the living room coffee table. He placed them in a small paper bag that went inside the pocket of his heavy coat.

Chapter Four

December 16 – 6:45 p.m.

Sam was late.

In fact, he was extremely late; and he knew he would never hear the end of it.

"Oh, you are in for it now! He's in one of his moods," Nurse Gray, a matronly black woman, warned. She placed a clipboard before him.

"I'm not afraid of him," Sam countered as he signed in, grinning. "He may still bark but he doesn't have any bite left."

"I wouldn't be too sure of that," she sniffed.

Sam made his way down the antiseptic hall to Leo's room, calling quiet greetings to the familiar faces he saw—two silver-haired ladies in wheelchairs.

"Good evening, Lyla, Merry Christmas! Happy Hannukah, Ann!"

Cautiously Sam poked his head into Leo's room. His friend appeared to be asleep in his hospitable-style bed. Lying there on his back with closed eyes he looked so frail, just a ghost of the robust man he once was. The years had not been as kind to Leo as they had to Sam. Four years prior the ravages of a stroke left him unable to care for himself, so his children put him in the nursing home and promptly forgot about their father.

Sam quietly slipped into the room and eased into one of the pair of the vinyl chairs next to Leo's bed. He didn't want to disturb Leo's nap. Looking fondly at his long-time friend, Sam thought back to better days.

The two young professors crouched behind the snow-laden bushes of the deserted campus waiting for their targets to come into range. As their unsuspecting wives rounded the corner of Compton Hall the snipers let their snowball missiles fly. The women shrieked with indignation at such an attack, but quickly retaliated with a barrage of their own.

Without warning an errant snowball smashed into the Dean's window shattering the glass with a loud crash. The foursome stared in horror as Dean Wilson's face appeared in the jagged opening. With a crook of his finger the Dean summoned them to his office.

Red-faced and dragging their feet the four entered the office.

"Dean Wilson, I'm sorry. It was my snowball that smashed the window," Sam said.

"No, Dean, I believe it was my snowball that broke the window," Leo claimed.

The Dean doubtfully raised his bushy white eyebrows and eyeballed his two young professors.

"This is not what I would consider appropriate behavior from my newest professors. Not necessarily the type of example the University wishes to set for its students. Somewhat juvenile don't you ladies agree?" he scowled at Irene and Sylvia.

Irene sidled over to Sam and slipped her hand into his. Squaring her shoulders, she bravely spoke up.

"Dean Wilson, Sam and Leo are fine examples of what this University stands for. We were just caught up in the fun of Christmas. We are sorry and we will certainly pay for the damage to your window."

The Dean again, albeit differently, raised his eyebrows at her passionate defense.

"Hmmm, since none of you seem to be sure whose snowball it was that broke my window, it wouldn't be fair to reprimand just one of you, now would it?"

Sam and Leo gulped audibly, both believing their teaching careers had come to an early, screeching halt. "Done in by snowballs, nonetheless; the humility of it all," Sam thought.

The Dean noticed their discomfort and paused for dramatic effect, slow to mete out his punishment.

"Since the four of you are so overcome with the holiday spirit I have the ideal restitution in mind. The Alumni Association is hosting a Christmas party for underprivileged children and we need a Santa Claus and several elves to help out.

The Dean's steady gleam as he sentenced the group communicated clearly that there was no room for discussion.

Sam looked quite snappy in his Santa suit, sadly though Leo made a none-too-attractive Christmas elf. But the party was a smashing success. For years after Sam continued to play Santa and Leo frequently made a welcome appearance as Sam's favorite elf.

Their friendship grew and strengthened. The couples were quite the foursome, until Sylvia's death nine years earlier. Now it was just the two of them, two lonely old men.

"It's about time you got here." Leo's slightly slurred growl jarred Sam's reminiscing. "How long were you going to sit there daydreaming?"

"I thought you were sleeping and I didn't want to disrupt your beauty rest."

"Sleeping? Ha, how could I sleep with all that racket you were making?" Leo countered.

"Racket? What are you talking about? I tip-toed in here as quiet as a church mouse."

"You may have tip-toed, but I heard your wheezing all the way from the nurse's station. You sound like an old pair of bellows." Leo chuckled at his clever analogy, his chest rising and falling. "And you're late! Some friend you are, not exactly Mr. Reliable! What's with you these days? You never used to be late."

"Complain all you want, you old coot, not even you can spoil my holiday mood! Roger and his family are coming for Christmas. It's going to be just like old times." Sam crowed.

As soon as he spoke those words Sam regretted them, realizing Leo's children would probably do little more than send a card. Leo's face was sullen.

"Ah Leo, I'm sorry. I shouldn't have said anything. It's just that..." Sam's voice trailed.

"You should be sorry, making me remember how miserable my life is. My kids don't have time for me," Leo said smugly.

"Leo, that's not true. Jim is in the service in England. He can't just go AWOL! You know how the military works. They need him there. And Judy has two small children to take care of. You remember how tough that is, especially when you're a single parent living halfway across the country. I'm sure you'll hear from both of them."

"Well, don't count on it." He paused and lifted his head from a lonely, far-away stare before perking up. "Let's see what you brought me and maybe I will forgive your sorry hide! What's in that bag you've got?" Leo's eyes twinkled with a hint of his old humor.

Sam levered himself out of the chair and walked to the open doorway. Sticking his head into the now vacant hallway, he looked both ways. Not spying a soul, he quickly pulled his head back into the room and quietly shut the door.

For obvious reasons Leo's door didn't have an interior lock so Sam slid a chair underneath the door handle. He cracked the window for ventilation. He drew the privacy curtain around Leo's bed. Leo didn't have a roommate, but the drawing of the curtain added to the moment's suspense. It was a scene they had played out many times.

"Hurry up! You've kept me waiting long enough," Leo demanded.

"Be quiet. Do you want the nurses to hear?" Sam admonished.

"Just open the damn bag, will you."

Sam shook his head over his friend's impatience. With a ceremonial flair he opened the paper sack and withdrew the awaited treasures—the small cough medicine bottle filled with scotch and a $5 cigar. Leo's eyes lit with anticipation as he watched Sam carefully pour out three fingers of the golden liquor into two paper cups. Sam handed one to Leo.

"To us Leo," Sam toasted.

"To us, Sam, Merry Christmas." Leo seconded as he lifted the cup to his mouth with a trembling hand, spilling a good portion of the scotch in the process. Sam pretended not to notice as he lit the cigar and passed it to his friend.

"Just a couple of puffs. We don't need you to have a coughing fit like last time. That will bring the nurses running for sure," Sam cautioned.

Leo closed his eyes and took a weak pull on the cigar and exhaled a thin stream of smoke.

"Ah, this ain't bad. Good scotch, a good cigar and an old friend—what else does a man need?" He paused and puffed again. "Give me another pull and I'll take back all the bad things I said about you." Leo smiled. Sam couldn't help but grin. He relented and poured him another. Leo looked seriously toward Sam. Hands shaking, he raised his cup. An anticipating Sam raised his.

"To our lovely, departed wives, we were so lucky to have them." quivered an emotional Leo.

"Ah...a fine toast, Leo. To our sweethearts! Gone but never forgotten! Salut!"

Sam and Leo emptied their cups. Leo again struggled. The two men sat quietly for a while, sharing the cigar. Leo broke the silence.

"So tell me about your holiday plans with your son. How did you talk him into coming home?"

"I didn't really have to talk him into it. It was actually Roger's idea. To tell you the truth, after the past couple of Christmases I was ready to cross December 25th right off the calendar. But you know, once Roger called to say they were coming home, something happened inside. I started to remember how great it had always been and I knew Irene would want me to have a good Christmas."

"We did have some great times," Leo agreed. "Remember the year Irene decided the four of us should host the church Christmas party? Boy did she ever work us like dogs!"

"The woman was ruthless," Sam laughed. "I think I peeled a couple hundred pounds of potatoes. Why I remember…"

"Sam you make the most handsome Santa," Irene said as she pressed her lips against his.

"Ah, I bet you say that to all the Santa Clauses," Sam chuckled.

"Only to the *real* one," she replied.

"Hey you two Christmas lovebirds, there are kids out there waiting for Santa to deliver their presents," Leo grumbled, looking ever so uncomfortable in his green elf suit with shiny pants and curled up shoes.

"Okay, okay, I'm ready. Let's go elfy. Nice legs, by the way," Sam joked as he walked into the church's small auditorium.

"Ho, Ho, Ho, Merry Christmas everyone! Merry Christmas!"

"Santa's here! He's here! Santa what did you bring me?" A chorus of excited young voices heralded Sam's entrance.

"One at a time, one at a time," Irene chided. "There are gifts for everyone."

Obediently the children formed a line and waited their turn. One-by-one they sat on Sam's lap and told him how good they had been and what their dearest wishes were. It was a wonderful time. Sam received countless thank yous as he handed each child a wrapped present. However, disaster loomed.

There were only five children left waiting to tell Santa what they hoped for and Sam knew he only had one present remaining in his bag. He improvised.

"Children, Santa will be right back. I have to check on my reindeer." Sam made a hasty exit to the back room. He pondered his predicament. "Oh damn!" he thought. "What am I going to do? I can't disappoint these kids."

A sudden handclasp on his shoulder and a soft "Ho, Ho, Ho," in his ear interrupted his worrying. Sam turned and discovered another Santa.

"Merry Christmas," the Santa said.

"Merry Christmas yourself," Sam replied.

"I wonder if maybe you could use a few extra presents?"

"I sure could. There are five more children out there and I only have one present left."

"Well then it seems that I am just in time," the Santa said as he handed Sam a beautiful red velvet sack.

"Oh, thanks so much. Merry Christmas to you."

"Merry Christmas to you, Sam. Now get out there and do your job."

Sam ho, ho hoed back to where the children anxiously waited for him. There were no disappointed youngsters that evening. Afterward, as Sam and Irene and Leo and Sylvia were cleaning up, Sam asked Irene if she knew the other Santa.

"What Santa?" she asked, offering an odd look. "You were the only Santa I saw tonight."

Neither Leo nor Sylvia had seen a second Santa. They too traded strange glances.

"Well whoever he was, he sure saved the day with those extra presents."

"Are you feeling alright, Sam?" Irene asked.

"I told him to stay off the eggnog," chided a smiling Leo. Sam gave Leo the evil eye. The smile vanished from Leo's face.

"Aw, forget it. Let's go home," Sam said as he scooped up a sleeping Roger.

"Come to think of it, I never did find out who that other Santa was. You know, I think I still have his sack somewhere in the attic," Sam recalled. "I'll have to see if I can find it to put the grandkids' gifts in."

A gentle rumbling startled Sam. He looked to his pal. At some point during his reminiscing Leo had fallen asleep. He began to lightly snore.

Sam stood and took the empty paper cup from Leo's clinging hand. Snuffing out the half-smoked cigar, Sam smiled sadly. Reaching out, he dusted the cigar ashes off of Leo's blanket, and contemplated how they shared so many wonderful memories. Sam felt that it was a shame for Leo and so many of the other nursing home residents to have to endure the holidays alone.

"So depressing," he thought. "I hope someone does something for these people." Sam closed the window and gathered the remains of their austere celebration. "I sure hope someone does something," he thought again as he left.

Chapter Five

December 18

Sam panicked as he scanned the mall parking lot searching for his parked car. He was sure he was in aisle 21—or was it aisle 12?

"Take a deep breath, old man," he muttered to himself. "No one stole your car. Who would want that old heap anyway?"

Row after row of dirty, salt-crusted cars attested to the fact that Sam wasn't the only last-minute Christmas shopper. The inside of the mall hadn't been any better. Harried shoppers surged through the stores, somewhat like lemmings to the sea, Sam thought.

Sam sorely missed the good ole' days when Christmas shopping was more of a gentle activity. In those days he and Irene strolled down Main Street, stopping at the hobby shop or the bookstore. Back then Sam understood the gifts he bought; model car sets, board games and footballs. But now, between computer programs, hand-held electronic games and designer T-shirts that coast as much as a good pair of shoes, Sam was baffled. Given the considerable sum of money he spent, the two shopping bags he toted seemed disturbingly light.

Sam stood on his tiptoes craning his neck to see into the next aisle. Belatedly, he remembered how Irene would always tie a ribbon to the car's antenna.

"Irene, Irene," Sam sighed. "Did I rely on you for everything?"

Sam could have sworn he heard her soft, laughing answer as he squeezed between two cars parked tighter than sardines in a can.

"Can I help you, sir?"

Startled, Sam turned to see that a mall security guard had driven up beside him in one of those little meter-maid carts.

"No thank you. I'm fine." Sam said.

"Are you sure?" the guard asked.

"Well, I sort of forgot where I parked my car," Sam sheepishly admitted.

"Hop in, I'll drive you around until we find it."

"Really?"

"Absolutely! That's what I'm here for."

Sam wedged himself into the small passenger's seat and clutched his two bags to his chest. He felt old and foolish having to be driven around to find his car.

"There it is," he exclaimed with relief. "Right where I parked it, in aisle six. I don't know why I thought I left it on aisle 21. I have been so busy these past few days. My son and his family are coming to visit for Christmas and between cleaning and shopping and decorating, well, I guess my age is showing."

"Don't worry about it. Believe me, age has nothing to do with it. It's just a crazy time of year. You would be surprised at how many people forget where they parked."

"Let me give you a little something for your help," Sam said as he struggled to reach for his wallet.

"That's not necessary, sir. I'm just happy to help. Merry Christmas and enjoy your family," the guard said with a smile.

"What a nice young fellow," Sam thought as he stowed his packages in the trunk. As he opened the car door a wave of dizziness washed over him. Knees buckling, Sam clutched the door, to keep his balance. After a few cautious moments the faintness passed and he was able to slide behind the wheel.

"I have to stop forgetting to take my medication," Sam thought. "You don't have time for this nonsense! Roger is coming home and you have a lot to do," he chastised himself as he turned the ignition. "Roger is coming home."

Chapter Six

December 19

The weatherman had predicted blizzard-like conditions for Madison, but the only area snowfall seemed to have occurred in Sam's kitchen. However, this blizzard was made of flour. A fine dust covered the countertops, the table, the floor and Sam himself. The sink was piled high with batter-sticky mixing bowls. Bits of cookie dough clung to the cabinets, refrigerator and even the window curtains. Nevertheless, what Sam lacked in baking skill he more than compensated for with enthusiasm.

A loud ding of the timer told Sam his latest batch of sugar cookies was ready. With great trepidation he opened the oven door.

"Whoopee!" he shouted as he lifted the baking sheet from its rack. "Perfection! We did it Badger, we did it!" Sam did a jig of joy around the kitchen table. "Third time's always a charm!" he crowed.

Badger, who up until this point had been a silent observer, meowed his disapproval of Sam's undignified dance. Deciding he had seen enough, the Tiger Stripe fled the kitchen, his regal exit tainted by tiny, floury paw prints.

Sam's first two attempts at creating the confections lay scattered in the backyard, a feast for the hungry birds. He had never given much thought to the amount of time and effort Irene put into baking Christmas cookies. She baked dozens and dozens for the neighbors, for the nursing home residents, and for whomever she thought could use a little holiday sweetness.

Sam had always thought that you just threw some flour and stuff in a bowl, mixed it up, popped it in the oven and voila—cookies! However, his baking results on this afternoon told a different story.

Sam picked up a still-hot, star-shaped cookie and carefully took a bite.

"Mmmm," murmured Sam as the buttery treat melted on his tongue. "Roger won't believe this!"

Sam spent the entire afternoon pouring over Irene's recipes and baking cookies. A good part of the evening was dedicated to cleaning the kitchen. Baking was hard, tiring work, Sam realized as he dried the last baking sheet.

Glancing at the clock, Sam was surprised to see that it was almost eight o'clock. He was going to have to pick up the pace tomorrow if he wanted to get things done before Roger came home.

"So much to do," Sam thought as he hung the dishtowel. "Tomorrow I'll buy the tree and finish decorating the house," he planned as he slowly climbed the stairs. "I better get a good night's rest. I've got a lot to do."

Chapter Seven

December 20

Sam pulled down the earflaps of his plaid lumberjack hat and wrapped his scarf tighter around his neck. Every year the cold seemed to seep into his bones a little quicker and deeper.

He stood in a forest of hewn pines, Douglas firs and blue spruces. Little trees, big trees, fat trees and skinny trees—the choices seemed endless. What was almost as startling as the selection of trees were the numbers on the price tags attached to each one. Sam looked at one tree's tag. It read $95.

"Surely that must be a mistake!" he thought. "There are pine trees all over Wisconsin, for heaven's sake! How on earth could a Christmas tree cost $95?"

Finally, too frozen to care, Sam selected a plump blue spruce. He gritted his teeth when the salesman said, "That'll be 45 bucks mister." But he opened his wallet and carefully retrieved two twenties and a five. The salesman tied the tree on top of Sam's car and moved on to fleece another customer.

Sam slowly drove home, mindful of the tree perched precariously atop his car. Along the way, he remembered all the times he, Irene and Roger had gone to buy a Christmas tree. They had always made an event of it. It was one of their favorite family traditions. However, which tree to buy was not always an easy decision. Invariably, they would each pick a different tree. Sam liked the big tall ones, Roger liked the short bushy ones, and Irene seemed to favor the scrawny little ones. After much laughter and good-natured debate Sam would always win, and year after year a big, tall Christmas tree graced their living room.

Sam backed into the driveway and got out of the car. Looking at the trussed tree, it seemed to him that somehow it had grown during the trip home. Using his pocketknife, he hacked the twine that secured it. The rope gave way and Sam half lifted and half slid the tree down.

Taking a firm grip on the lower branches, he slowly dragged the tree along the walkway to the front porch. A fine perspiration mist broke on his brow as he laboriously thumped the tree up the stairs. Grunting with exertion, Sam finally reached the top step.

"I'll take a pill when I get this danged tree in the house," Sam promised himself.

He unlocked the front door and pushed it wide open. Bracing his feet against the sill-plate, Sam gave a final heave and he and the tree tumbled into the foyer.

Lying on the floor with pine branches poking him here and there, Sam laughed. It was one of those silly bouts of laughter, the kind where you're not really sure what you are laughing about, but you just can't seem to stop.

Wiping at the tiny tears that leaked from his eyes, Sam struggled to free himself from the branches. As he stood, another pain lanced through his chest. Fumbling through his pocket, Sam found his pillbox and quickly slipped a tablet beneath his tongue.

"I don't have time for this," Sam thought as he waited for the pill to work its magic. "There's too much to do. Roger will be here in three days."

Chapter Eight

December 22

Listening to Christmas music on his old RCA 78" vinyl record player, Sam carefully finished drying a dinner plate. He spent the entire afternoon washing dishes, polishing silver and cleaning the house. It was hard work trying to do all of the things Irene had done for the family. She always made sure that everything was perfect, down to the smallest detail.

"Let's see," he mused. "What to do next? Change the linens or wrap presents?"

Before he could decide, the ringing of the phone interrupted his thoughts.

"Hello and Merry Christmas," Sam said as he answered the telephone.

"Hello, Dad. It's Roger."

"Roger it's good to hear your voice. Just think in less than 24 hours you will be here! I've made cookies and right now I was getting ready to…"

"Dad, slow down. I've got some bad news."

"Bad news? Are you and the kids okay?"

"We're all fine, Dad. It's Kate's mom. She had a stroke and is in intensive care. Kate can't leave her alone right now."

Sam made no sound, unless of course the sound of one's heart breaking is audible.

"Dad, are you there? Dad, answer me," Roger's worried voice broke through Sam's disappointment.

"Yes, I'm here son."

"Dad, I am so sorry. Please say you will come out here. I'll call the airlines and have a ticket ready for you. I don't want you to spend Christmas alone," Roger pleaded.

"No Roger, it's alright. You're going to have your hands full. Kate needs you. You don't need another old person under foot. I'll be fine here, son. Take care of your family."

"Dad you won't be any trouble. You know Jenna and Chris really want to see you. They were so excited about the visit."

There was a short pause.

"Flying doesn't agree with me, Roger."

"Are you sure, Dad? It won't be the same without you."

"I know, I know, Roger. But these things happen. You have your own family to see to," Sam said, trying to maintain a brave façade.

"We'll come for Easter. I promise. I love you Dad." Roger's voice was thick with emotion.

"I love you too, son. I love you too. Tell Kate I'll pray for her mother and hug the kids for me too. Merry Christmas to everyone..."

Sam slowly hung up the phone. In a few short minutes his joy was shattered. He knew in his head that Roger was doing what was right for his family, but in his heart he was disappointed and hurt.

Tears stung Sam's eyelids as he crossed the kitchen to the cabinet that held Leo's scotch. Sam had found some empty solace in the same bottle after Irene died and he again hoped for the same numbness.

With an unsteady hand Sam poured a shot of scotch whiskey. He raised the small glass to his lips and with a quick motion of his head he threw down the contents. His throat burned, his lungs shuddered, and his stomach clenched as the powerful liquid traveled its course.

He poured himself another. This time before he swallowed, he held some of the liquor in his mouth, relishing the fiery sensation it brought. Gulping and wheezing, he finished the drink. The third shot went down easily.

"I can't believe this is happening. They're not coming. They're not coming!" Sam moaned as he shuffled into the living room. The well-lit Christmas tree he had so lovingly decorated just days ago, now glowed garishly. The wreath, the lights, the candles, the tinsel, everything, all of it—looked out of place. The room's holiday spirit seemed to mock his anguish.

Sam stumbled, felt slippers slapping. Tears streamed down his booze-flushed face as he stood in front of the tree. He reached out a trembling finger to touch the Popsicle stick snowflake. Misery consumed his body and he began tearing the tinsel from the tree, throwing it on the floor. Fragile glass balls made melancholy tinkling sounds as they broke.

Sobbing, he cried out, "That's it, no more Christmas! There will never be another Christmas as long as I live. There will be no more Christmas!"

Suddenly Sam's hand stilled as he heard another voice, this one echoing in his memory. It was his mother's voice harshly choking out the same words, "There will be no Christmas this year or any other year…"

Nine-year-old Sam stared at his mother in disbelief, watching in horror as her hands cruelly tore the ornaments from the tree.

"Mama, what do you mean there will be no more Christmas? Christmas is in two days. Stop it, stop it," Sam pleaded.

"I meant what I said. There will be no Christmas! They just called from the hospital. Your father is dead!"

Three weeks earlier, Sam's father had been injured in an accident at work. The doctors weren't sure if he would recover, but no one had expected him to die just two days before Christmas.

Sam frantically tried to stop her before she destroyed all of the decorations they'd prepared.

"Mama, stop, please! We have to have Christmas. Daddy loves Christmas! He says it's his favorite time of the year."

Sam's mother collapsed to her knees, her grief a tangible thing. She held her head in the palms of her hands crying. Rubbing her back, Sam was desperate to console her.

"It will be okay, Mama. We can have Christmas. I have presents for you and Jerry and Emily and…" Sam's voice trailed off as the impact of his mother's words slammed into his heart.

"No, no. He isn't dead. He will be here. He loves Christmas," Sam sobbed.

"Your father is dead. He's gone! There will be no more Christmas! Throw the presents out. Burn them! I don't care. He's gone!" She sobbed uncontrollably.

A tearful, sniffling Sam gathered up the four presents that he had a day earlier wrapped and placed under the tree. With one last look at his weeping mother he ran from the house. He ran and ran until finally his burning lungs would let him run no more.

Dropping to the snowy ground, Sam curled protectively around his precious bundles. Sobbing with the tortured confusion of a child shown the painful truth of life, Sam did not realize he was not alone.

"What's the matter big fellow?" a kindly voice asked.

Sam drew in a shuddering breath and looked up through tear-blurred eyes to see, of all people, Santa! But no, this couldn't be Santa, he thought, Christmas was still two days away.

"Go away! You're not the real Santa Claus! You can't help me."

"I look like Santa, don't I?"

"Well," Sam hesitated. He did look like Santa. He had shiny black boots and a bright red coat and his curly white beard looked real, unlike the Santa at the church party last week.

"You don't look too convinced. Why don't you tell me about it Sam, and maybe I can help." The old man smiled and his eyes twinkled.

Sam sat up, drew his coat sleeve under his running nose and said with a hiccup, "My dad died."

"Oh my, that is a terrible thing," Santa said with a sad look in his eyes.

"He got hurt at work and he didn't get better. My mama is very mad. She is crying and tearing down the Christmas tree. She says we can't have Christmas this year or ever again." Tears rolled down Sam's cheeks.

Santa sat down and pulled Sam gently onto his lap. Rocking the sobbing child, the old man crooned soothing words.

"Oh Sam, your father dying is almost the saddest thing your mother could imagine, and because he loved Christmas so much, she can't imagine celebrating it without him."

Sam stopped sniffling for a moment, sat up, and looked at Santa.

"My daddy really isn't coming back, is he?" Sam whispered.

"No Sam, he isn't. But he will always be in your heart and in your thoughts. I know you love him and will miss him, and it's okay to cry if you want."

Sam's lip quivered, but he resisted shedding another tear. He wiped his eyes with the back of his other sleeve.

"He said this Christmas was going to be really special, because I was gonna be his helper. I was gonna help him give out the presents."

"Well Sam, your daddy must have thought you were very grown up if he was going to let you be his Christmas helper," Santa said.

"And now we ain't even gonna have Christmas," Sam said quietly.

"Ah, Sam, let me tell you a little secret that really isn't a secret at all. Christmas isn't about one day once a year. Christmas is about feeling kindness and love all year long. So just for this one holiday season, your family feels too sad to celebrate, but the wonderful feeling of Christmas will come back. You and your family will be able to remember your father and how much he loved Christmas without feeling like you want to cry. Do you understand?" Santa looked at Sam hoping that the young boy would find some comfort in his words.

"What am I going to do with the presents that I have?"

Sam slid off Santa's lap and picked up the four slightly-crushed packages from the ground.

"I have one for Mama, one for Jerry, one for Emily and one for Daddy."

Sam smoothed the crumpled wrapping on each present as he spoke.

"I saved my money for a long time and I bought Mama a lace hanky. I got Jerry a yo-yo and I got jacks for Emily."

"That was thoughtful of you Sam," Santa said tenderly.

"Wanna see what I made for Daddy?" Sam asked. "The paper is kinda ripped so it doesn't matter if you open it, I guess."

Brows furrowed, Sam carefully unwrapped the gift. Lifting it with both hands, he proudly showed it to Santa.

"Why Sam, it's a work of art," Santa said.

"I made it myself. It's a tie holder."

Santa took the prized present from Sam to admire it more closely. Sam had glued an odd assortment of empty thread spools to a piece of wood and then had painstakingly painted each one a different color.

"Your father would have loved this gift. He would be so proud to have such a wonderful tie holder."

For a moment Sam beamed with pride, then he remembered.

"What am I gonna do with all this stuff? Mama says throw em' out, but I don't wanna." Tears threatened again as Sam looked to Santa for help.

"Sam, I think you should save your Mama's and Jerry's and Emily's presents until next Christmas. Just tuck them away in your closet."

"I guess I could do that. But what about my Daddy's present?" Sam asked as he cradled the tie holder.

"I have an idea. Remember you told me that this year you were going to be your father's special helper?"

Sam nodded.

"Would you like to be my helper this year? You could be Santa's helper."

"I could? What would I do?"

"Well, I know someone who would be very happy to get such a wonderful gift as your tie holder."

Sam looked skeptically at Santa.

"Give my Daddy's tie holder to somebody else?"

"I know you made it especially for your father, but I know a nice old gentleman who doesn't have anyone to bring him a Christmas present this year."

"Nobody at all?" Sam asked.

"No one. Not any children or grandchildren; he is all alone this year."

"And you think he would like my tie holder?"

"I know he would think it was the most special gift in the whole wide world," Santa said smiling.

"Well, I guess so…" Sam said, warming to the idea. "But I get to put my name on it, right? So he knows it's from me?"

"You can sign the tag Santa's helper Sam."

Santa told Sam about Mr. Park, a lonely retired widower who had no children. Sam knew who Mr. Park was. He walked past his house everyday on his way to school.

"I didn't know he was lonely," Sam said.

"He is, Sam; especially at Christmas time. So what do you say, do you think you would like to give Mr. Park your tie holder?"

Sam thought about it for a few seconds. His eyes welled with tears when he thought about not seeing his father again.

"I don't know," he said.

"It's your decision Sam, but I think your father would be proud of you if you tried to make someone else a little happy. You know, I even think it will make you feel happy too." Santa paused. "Remember this, Sam, and one day you'll fully understand the *true* meaning of Christmas.

"Okay, but I need to wrap it again."

"Let's see if we can fix it."

Santa and Sam carefully wrapped the crumpled paper around the tie holder and tied it with the ribbon. Santa magically produced a piece of paper and a pencil and Sam wrote, "To Mr. Park from Santa's helper Sam."

"Can I give it to him today?"

"I think that would be a great idea. But then you need to go home, Sam. Your mother will start worrying about you."

"Okay."

Sam stared at the ground, scuffing the toe of his boot in the snow.

"Santa?"

"Yes Sam?"

"How will the real Santa know not to come to our house on Christmas Eve?" Sam earnestly asked.

"The real Santa?" Santa replied, raising his bushy white brows. "Who do you think I am?"

"Aw come on, I know you're not the real Santa. You're just one of his helpers, like me. The real Santa is way too busy to be here today," Sam countered with a child's conviction.

"Don't worry Sam. Santa knows. He knows. Now go deliver that present and take care of your mama."

"Okay, I will. Merry Christmas, uh, Santa!"

"Don't forget Mr. Park," Santa called as Sam ran off. "Merry Christmas, Sam, Merry Christmas."

Sam ran all the way to Mr. Park's house and up the porch steps. He stood nervously at the front door, shifting his weight from side to side. He had never been to Mr. Park's house and he was feeling a little unsure, but Santa's words about how proud his father would be gave Sam the courage to knock on the door. He rapped three times. At first Mr. Park didn't answer, so Sam knocked harder the second time.

"Mr. Park are you home? It's me Sam Adams."

The door cracked open to a creaky voice.

"Who is it?"

"Sam Adams, Mr. Park. I'm your neighbor from down the street. I have something for you."

"Sam Adams? Oh yes, I've seen you."

The front door opened wider.

"What you doin' here?" Mr. Park asked.

Sam's bottom lip trembled slightly as he held out the package.

"I have a Christmas present for you. I'm Santa's helper Sam and I know you don't have anybody to give you a Christmas present so this was for my Daddy but he died, so Santa said I should give it to you because it will make you happy and my Daddy would be proud of me," Sam struggled as the words all ran together.

"Your father died? I heard he was in the hospital…I'm sorry Sam." Mr. Park said. His eyes grew misty. He took the gift and with great reverence opened the corrected packaging, revealing the tie holder.

"Sam, this is the most wonderful gift I've ever received," whispered the old man. His throat was tight with emotion.

"It's a tie holder," Sam offered.

"Well, it is most likely the best tie holder in the entire world! Thank you Sam."

"Merry Christmas, Mr. Park." Sam smiled.

"Thank you and Merry Christmas, Sam," said Mr. Park, returning the smile.

Sam bounced down Mr. Park's steps two at a time and headed home. As he ran, he realized that Santa was right—that he did feel a little happy, and for the moment the pain of his father's death was stilled by the joy of Christmas.

Chapter Nine

"Dear heavens," Sam breathed as he looked down at the torn tinsel and decorations in his hands. "I forgot. I forgot what Christmas is really all about! All I could think of was myself."

Sam staggered to the sofa and lowered himself onto the soft cushions. With a hoarse sob he buried his face in his hands. He felt the childhood pain of his father's death as if it were yesterday, instead of more than 65 years ago. Emotions rushed through him, spurring an onslaught of hitherto faded memories. He remembered the funeral and his mother's sobs of grief. He remembered his brother and sister's confusion and his own deep sense of loss. But as strong as those painful memories now were, he still remembered the remarkable feeling of bringing happiness to someone despite his own sadness.

Years of happy Christmas memories coursed through him. The night he met Irene at the Christmas party; the times he played Santa at the children's hospital; Roger's first Christmas; the food baskets they delivered to needy families, his buddy, Leo. The happy memories seemed endless. But the happiness did end. It ended that horrible night three years earlier when Irene passed.

"Oh, Irene—why did you have to leave me?" Sam sobbed into tinsel-laced fingers. "I always thought that I would go first!"

Sam knew he had spent the last two years pretending: Pretending to smile, pretending to enjoy Christmas at Roger's house and pretending to listen to his neighbor's problems. But Sam knew the biggest pretense of all was his belief that if only Roger came home for Christmas that everything would be like it was before.

The soft push-push of kneading cat paws broke through Sam's despair. Sam lifted his head from his hands and looked down at Badger.

"Ah, old fellow, at least I still have you. What would I do without you?"

Badger purred like a rusty motor as Sam scratched his furry cat's ears and lovingly stroked the length of his back.

"We've got a lot of work to do Badger. It's about time I started believing in Christmas again," Sam said. "Did I ever tell you about the time I met Santa? No? Well, I was nine and…"

Chapter Ten

With Christmas Eve only a day away Sam knew he didn't have much time to put a plan into action. The first order of business was to find his old Santa suit. He had not worn it for five or six years, but he knew it was in the attic somewhere.

Sam flipped on the light switch and slowly climbed the narrow attic stairway. At the top of the steps he paused to catch his breath. The room was crammed with boxes of memories. Irene had a hard time parting with anything that she considered a sentimental keepsake.

"It's strange that my suit wasn't with all the other Christmas stuff. I don't even know where to begin; I could be up here for days," Sam thought as he started his search. Badger joined in the hunt, stealthily stalking the dust motes that danced in the glow of the overhead light bulb.

"Well, I'll be," Sam murmured. Not sure whether it was luck or fate that drew him to the attic's far corner, he opened a large box, and there it was—his Santa suit. Irene had carefully wrapped it in tissue paper.

Smiling, Sam took the jacket out of the box and gave it a shake. Holding it up against his chest, Sam could see that the coat was a little worse for the wear. The velvet, once a bright crimson, had faded to a dull red and the once-white trim was now a dingy gray.

Neatly folding the jacket and setting it aside, Sam reached back in the box and drew out his Santa trousers, cap, wig and beard. It was all there.

"Ah Irene, my little pack-rat" Sam whispered affectionately. "I could always count on you."

Sam put the costume back into the carton and with a grunt lifted the box. He turned to make his way to the stairs when he tripped and nearly fell.

"What the heck?" he remarked as he glanced down to see what had caused his stumble. "How did this get here?" he wondered aloud, looking at the small white box lying directly in his path. He had not noticed it before.

He nudged the parcel with his toe and the lid fell off revealing a bit of bright red fabric. Sam set down the box that he was holding and stooped to further inspect the contents of the mysterious carton.

Inside was a Santa sack, the brilliant red-velvet sack looked brand new. Immediately Sam remembered. It was the sack from the Santa that had saved the day at the Church Christmas party years ago. He held it up and noticed it was in perfect condition. "Well, this will come in handy," Sam thought as he tucked it under his arm. Glancing at his watch, he saw that the hour was getting late.

"Come on Badger," he called. "Let's go make some dinner while we figure out what to do next."

At Sam's call, the cat abandoned his prowling and the dusty duo made their way down the stairs.

Chapter Eleven

December 24 – 7 a.m.

Sam awoke Christmas Eve morning no differently than he had every morning for the past two years. He kept his eyes squeezed tightly shut and held his breath. By doing this he could trick himself into believing that he could feel Irene snuggled at his side. At times, he could even sense the gentle rise and fall of her breath as it tickled his neck.

Sometimes the feeling only lasted a few seconds, and those mornings were particularly hard on Sam. Other days, Sam had to slide a tentative foot over to Irene's side of the bed to make sure she really wasn't there.

This Christmas Eve morning was a good one; Sam knew that Irene was with him, proud of what he was about to do and providing him with tender encouragement.

"I've got to get up and get going, Irene. I have an awful lot of things to do today," Sam whispered to her nightstand picture. "Lots to do."

Sam hastily dressed and hurried downstairs. He was quite a sight with his bristly white chin and sparse hair poking up in all directions.

"What to do first? What to do first?" Sam chanted as he set the teakettle on the burner. "Let's see, Sadie Cohen, and little Jason, oh and I can't forget Barbara Donavan and her family," Sam thought as he generously spooned instant coffee into his cup, briskly stirring as he continued his planning.

"I probably should visit Leo first, who knows what time those old folks hit the sack," Sam decided as he took a sip of his coffee.

"Ugh," he said, grimacing at the bitter brew taste.

Sam quickly stuffed a bite of dry bread into his mouth. He gulped a couple of mouthfuls of the dreadful coffee to wash down the stale bread.

"Some breakfast," he thought. "Well, no time to make anything better. I've got to get going."

He turned to pour the remaining coffee into the sink. However, Badger's hearty yowl let Sam know that there was another mouth to feed.

"Hey there old fellow! Reminding me to feed you breakfast, are you? I've got a lot to do, but be sure I'd never forget you!" Sam said as he filled his pet's bowl. Badger immediately devoured his food.

"I'd better make a list so I don't forget anything else."

Sam sat at the kitchen table and made his list and checked it twice. He was careful to make sure he wouldn't miss a thing.

Chapter Twelve

December 24
6 p.m.

"Mr. Adams, what a surprise. I didn't expect to see you here tonight." Nurse Gray exclaimed. "I thought you would be home celebrating Christmas Eve with your family."

"Ah, unfortunately there was a change of plans. My son and his family weren't able to make the trip. So I came to visit Leo."

"That's a shame about your family. But, I'm glad you came to see Leo. He really could use some company. He's a tough old coot, but the holidays really get to him. He hasn't heard one word from his kids," the nurse said.

"Well I've got just the thing to cheer him up," Sam said as he lifted two large shopping bags with rope handles. "Do you think we could get him in a wheelchair?" he asked.

"Actually, I think he is in his chair. Last time I saw him one of the aides had taken him to the Rec Room to watch a Christmas video. Do you want to visit him there or should I have someone bring him back to his room?" she offered.

"No, no, leave him with the others. I'll go see him there. I just need to stop in his room for a minute."

"Go right ahead Mr. Adams," she said with a nod.

Sam walked down the hall again whistling "Jingle Bells," barely noticing how heavy the shopping bags were.

"I wonder what he's up to?" Nurse Gray pondered as she watched him saunter cheerfully down the hallway. "Well, whatever it is, Leo will be glad to see him."

Sam slipped into Leo's room and quietly closed the door. He dumped the contents of the first shopping bag on to the bed. The red Santa outfit tumbled out. Sam quickly dressed into the trousers and coat and sat on the bed's edge to tug on his heavy black boots. After a brief struggle the boots slid on.

"Whew," Sam panted as he paused to catch his breath. "Getting old, Sam, getting old," he muttered to himself.

Snatching the wig and beard from the bed, Sam walked to the mirror to apply the finishing touches. Peering at his reflection, Sam was quite pleased with his appearance.

"You look like the real McCoy, old fellow," he said to himself.

Plopping his red cap atop the curly white wig, Sam felt his transformation was complete.

"Ho, ho, ho, Merry Christmas," he said.

"No, that's not right," he thought. "Too weak."

"Ho, ho, ho! Merry Christmas!" he boomed, the effect spoiled by a racking cough.

"Well, we'll have to find a happy medium," he thought. "Santa can't sound like he has the croup."

Sam stuffed his street clothes into the empty shopping bag and hid it under the bed. Rummaging through the other shopping bag Sam pulled out two large tins of his homemade sugar cookies and a somewhat rumpled elf's cap complete with a large red plume.

With one last look in the mirror and a final beard adjustment, Sam was ready. Picking up the cookie tins and the hat, he was ready to begin his rounds.

Sam opened the door and peered into the hallway. Both directions were clear. No one was in sight.

Sam quietly made his way down the hallway. He could hear the muffled sounds of a television coming from the Rec Room. He hesitated outside the doorway and took a deep breath. He was a little nervous and his heart raced, but he felt wonderful.

"Ho, ho, ho! Merry Christmas!" his voice thundered without a crack. "Merry Christmas everyone! Santa is here!"

The nursing home residents, who had been watching "It's A Wonderful Life," looked up with varying degrees of surprise. After a few seconds of stunned silence the room erupted with gasps of astonishment and chuckles of joy.

"Merry Christmas, Merry Christmas!" Sam called. "I have a treat for everyone, but I'm going to need a little assistance from my special helper, Elf Leo. Where are you old fellow?"

"Over here, Santa," answered Leo. His eyes sparkled. "Push me over there and be quick about it," Leo snapped at a smiling aide. The aide rolled Leo over to Sam.

"Hold these, will you Elfy?" Sam asked. His wide grin was only partially obscured by the bushy white beard.

Sam set the two cookie tins in Leo's lap. Leo grasped them firmly with his good hand. Sam plopped the elf cap on Leo's head and adjusted its brim at a jaunty angle. Sam bent down and whispered in Leo's ear, "Are you feeling up to this old fellow?"

Leo looked up at Sam with a lopsided grin. His eyes brimmed with happy tears.

"Are you kidding? This is just like old times! Let's get this Christmas show on the road!" Leo said. His voice was stronger and surer than it had been in months. "We've got a lot of ground to cover."

"Ladies and gentlemen, Santa and his elf, Leo, have a treat for you. Homemade Christmas cookies," Sam announced to the delighted audience. "No shoving now, there are plenty for everyone."

Sam slowly wheeled Leo around the room offering cookies to everyone.

"You make a mighty mangy-looking elf," one man hooted at Leo.

"I think he's handsome," a tiny, gray-haired woman retorted.

The residents crowded around the Christmas duo, all wanting to be part of the small festivity. Sam made sure that no one was forgotten.

"Come on elf," Sam said. "We need to visit those people who are in their rooms."

"Merry Christmas everyone," Sam shouted.

"Merry Christmas Santa, Merry Christmas elf," the group chorused.

Sam wheeled Leo into the hall.

"Which way Elf?"

"To Margaret's room, I want to make sure she gets some cookies."

"Oh, ho! What have we here?" Sam queried. "Is there something special about this particular lady?"

"Humph," Leo replied. "She's lonely that's all. This is her first year here and I know how she feels."

"Your wish is my command, elf," Sam chuckled as he whisked Leo down the hallway.

What a sight the two of them were, Sam dressed in his slightly threadbare Santa suit and Leo with his crooked grin and hat to match. They whooped and hollered like a couple of youngsters. It seemed to Sam that he had wings on his heels as they flew down the hallways calling Merry Christmas and offering cookies to all. They were greeted first with gasps of surprise, sometimes bordering on downright shock, which quickly gave way to grins of happiness. The pair's joy was infectious.

Sam was glad he made over six dozen of Irene's cookies. Everyone loved them. They continued on their mission, visiting every room-bound resident. Upon finishing, they headed toward Leo's room. As they passed the nurse's station, Nurse Gray spoke up.

"Hey guys! How did it go?" she asked.

"Very well, thanks." Sam replied. "We're just finishing up."

"Excellent! What perfect timing. Leo, you have a phone call. Would you like to take it in your room?"

Leo appeared shocked. Nevertheless, his pale expression quickly turned to anticipation.

"Yes. Take me in there, Sam," he replied.

"Sure thing, Elfy!"

Sam wheeled him into his room next to the phone. Leo picked up the receiver.

"Hello?"

Sam watched intently.

"Hi dad! Merry Christmas!" said Judy, his daughter.

"Judy! Merry Christmas! Is it ever wonderful to hear your voice!"

Leo smiled and looked to Sam. Sam smiled and quietly exited, leaving Leo alone.

Another voice entered the phone conversation.

"Hey dad! Merry Christmas from England!"

"Jim? Is that you? Are you in Texas too?"

"No dad!" Jim said, laughing heartily, "I'm still across the pond, in England! This is a conference call! Judy and I planned this!"

"My God, it's like we're all together!" said Leo.

Minutes later Leo opened the door to his room. Sam, standing by the nurse's station with his beard pulled down, noticed.

"How's that for a Christmas surprise? And you thought they wouldn't call! They double-teamed you! How about that modern technology?"

Beaming proudly, Leo could not contain his happiness.

"Judy is pregnant again with a girl and Jim is finally getting married!"

Leo paused and Sam registered the excitement with a huge grin.

"Can you believe it? What a Christmas gift!"

Sam walked to Leo, who was in his wheelchair, and patted him on the shoulder.

"Old friend, I'm happy for you. Now, I've got to be going. I have a few more deliveries to make tonight and it's getting late."

Sam still had his hand on Leo's shoulder. Leo grabbed it so he couldn't leave.

"Wait a minute…I want to…" Leo's voice cracked as he started to talk.

"What's wrong? Are you alright?" Sam asked in a worried tone.

Leo grabbed Sam's arm and pulled him down to look into his eyes.

"Thank you, Sam."

"For what?"

"For this…for remembering what Christmas *really* is, and for sharing that memory with me. I haven't felt this good since, well you know what, I can't even remember when. You're a good man Sam Adams, and most of all, a darn good friend! Thank you."

Leo breathed deeply. "Matter of fact, next to my dear wife Sylvia, you are the best friend I ever had. I just wanted you to know that, you old son-of-a-gun!"

Fighting back tears, Sam composed himself.

"Hey? What's with the speech? Sounds like a eulogy!"

"I just wanted you to know, that's all! You got something in your eyes? They look kinda' drippy to me. You're not getting all sappy, are you?"

Sam shook his head. He looked affectionately at the man who had been his best friend for over 50 years.

"Yeah, Leo. Something is in my eye. It must be lint from that moldy old hat you're wearing!"

"Bah! Call me an aide. I want to get back to the Rec Room. One of the little old ladies back there said I looked 'handsome' in this old elf hat! Merry Christmas old friend!…Aide! Aide!"

Sam watched as the aide wheeled Leo down the hall.

"Merry Christmas, old fellow, Merry Christmas," he whispered.

"That was a wonderful thing you did, Mr. Adams."

Sam turned to see Nurse Gray smiling at him.

"It was nothing, really."

"No, it was something special. I haven't seen Leo that happy. And the others, well they'll be talking about Santa and his elf for days."

"Merry Christmas, Ms. Gray," said a blushing Sam.

"Merry Christmas, Santa." She kissed his cheek.

Sam walked out of the nursing home into the blustery night air. He looked at his watch, and was surprised to find that it was almost eight o'clock. The day was flying by and he still had much to do.

He opened his car door and slid into the driver's seat. He lowered his head onto the steering wheel and rested. After a couple of minutes, he sat up and absently rubbed the dull ache in his chest.

"Whew, can't slow down. Got too much to do," he said aloud.

The car protested, but finally started. Sam carefully backed out of the parking space and pulled out the lot. As he drove home, he mentally reviewed his list of things still to do.

"It's going to be a long night, that's for sure. Ah, Santa's work is never done," he thought with a smile, "Never done."

Chapter Thirteen

December 24 – 8:30 p.m.

Sam pulled to a stop in front of Sadie Cohen's house. Peering through the windshield, he could see light shining from the downstairs windows. But something looked odd about the place, something about the windows themselves.

"Why they're barred!" Sam realized with dismay. "Poor Sadie had bars put on her windows! What is the world coming to?" he thought as he exited his car. Rounding the rear of the auto, he opened the backseat passenger door and hoisted out his portable television set.

Sam wished that he'd had the time, money and energy to buy Sadie a new TV.

"It's the thought that matters the most, isn't it?" he ruminated.
The 13-inch TV set wrapped with a red ribbon Sam carried up the steps had just recently graced the small side table in his den.

"Ah, I don't watch it all that often anyway," he said. "Sadie sure will enjoy it more than I do."

Sam put the point of his elbow against the doorbell and leaned into the button. He heard musical chimes echo inside Sadie's foyer. A few seconds later the porch light came on, forcing Sam to squint against the sudden brightness.

"Who's there? Who is it?" came a high-pitched voice.
Sam could see Sadie's face peeking difficultly through the curtains on the door's window.

"It's me, Sadie, Sam Adams," he replied.

"Who? What do you want?" Sadie's voice quaked.

Sam suddenly remembered that he was dressed like Santa, including a wig and beard.

"No wonder she doesn't recognize me," he thought.

Balancing the television on one lifted knee, Sam reached up with his free hand and pulled the beard from his chin.

"It's Sam Adams, Sadie. You remember, Irene's husband!"

Sam could see Sadie's eyes blink in surprise.

"Sam? Sam Adams, is it really you? What on earth are you doing here dressed up like that?"

"I came to wish you Merry Christmas, Sadie! And I have a little present here for you."

"Merry Christmas? Sam what are you talking about? I'm Jewish!" Sadie exclaimed.

Sam could hear her unlocking the various bolts and chains that helped her feel safe in her own home. He hoped they gave her some comfort.

"Did you hear me Sam? I'm Jewish, we don't celebrate Christmas and Hanukkah is over," she said as she fully opened the front door. Sam saw she was in her robe and slippers.

"Well, Sadie, today I am Santa's helper Sam, and I understand that you could use a little holiday spirit. So look what I have here for you," Sam said as he held up the TV. "Now I know it's not brand-spanking-new, but this old model still has a lot of life in it. Whatta ya say? Do you think you could use a television?" Sam's arms were starting to ache and he hoped that Sadie would hurry up with her answer.

"Oh Sam," she said, with her hands to her mouth and fighting back tears. It was her only reply, and it was the answer he'd hoped for.

"Where shall I put it, Sadie?"

Chapter Fourteen

Sam stood in his driveway and scratched his head, pondering the situation. There was no way that he could lift the Christmas tree onto his car's rooftop. He certainly couldn't do it without breaking a couple of the tree's limbs and maybe even a couple of his own in the process. Besides, he had to account for all the decorations and lights that now hung from the tree's branches.

"Ah ha," he thought as he crunched through the snow up the driveway to the garage. "I have just the solution!"

Sam went into the garage and flipped on the overhead light.

"I know it's in here somewhere," he muttered, pushing several junk items aside.

"Yes!" he exclaimed triumphantly as he spotted his quarry. "This will work just fine!"

Ten minutes later Sam walked Dunbar Street pushing his holiday cargo in an old wheelbarrow rusted with small holes. A tinsel trail glittered on the sidewalk in his wake.

It was quite a trek to the Donovan's home, but Sam kept his pace, whistling a tune to try and distract himself from the pain in his chest and the burning of his leg muscles.

Sam wasn't exactly sure why he had made the decision to give Barbara Donovan his Christmas tree. Maybe it was because he was worried that on Christmas morning he would be too sad about Roger not coming home to enjoy it, or maybe it was because it just looked so pretty that he wanted to share it with Barbara and her family. Whatever his reason, he was confident it was one that Irene would understand.

By the time Sam reached his destination, he was quite winded. Looking up the steps at the front of the house, Sam knew he would never be able to carry the tree up to the door. He thought, "But if I can't carry it up the steps, how will Barbara be able to? Bob isn't able to help her, and I don't want to spoil the surprise for her children."

Sam took a deep breath and said aloud, "Come on old man, what are you—some kind of wimp? You can do it!"

He gingerly tipped the wheelbarrow to its side and let the tree slide gently to the sidewalk. A couple of glass ornaments fell unnoticed on the lawn. Gritting his teeth, Sam lifted the tree and slowly maneuvered it up the front steps, shedding more ornaments and tinsel as he went. Finally, he made it to the top.

"Whew," Sam panted. He was tired, but pleased with himself, nonetheless.

Sam steadied the tree on its stand and reached out a hand to rap on the door. He hesitated. A niggling feeling made him glance at the tree.

"How did I miss this?" he asked himself as he plucked an ornament from one of the upper limbs. His eyes misted as he examined the coveted Popsicle stick snowflake.

"This goes home with me," he thought as he tucked the sentimental snowflake ornament Roger had made for him into his Santa coat.

Raising a gloved hand, he rapped again soundly on the front door. After no answer, he turned to leave.

Before he reached the bottom step, he heard Barbara's voice call out as she opened the door.

"Santa? What's this? Who are you?"

Sam looked back at her baffled expression. He couldn't help but chuckle.

"Ho, ho, ho! Merry Christmas, Barbara! I understand that you've been a very good girl this year and I thought that you and your family could use a little Christmas cheer!"

Barbara wore a puzzled look.

"Is that you, Sam Adams, underneath the beard?"

"Heavens no! Tonight I'm Santa's helper, Sam."

"Mr. Adams…"

"Aha, Santa's-helper-Sam, if you please."

Barbara laughed aloud at Sam's sincerity.

"Well, what can I do for you, Santa's-helper-Sam?" she asked.

"Now, now Barbara, I don't need anything. In fact, I have something for you and your family." Sam said as he gestured toward the tree. "I hope you will enjoy it."

Barbara gasped as she saw the tree for the first time.

"My goodness! This tree, it's so…Oh it's just beautiful! Thank you… *Santa*."

"I know your children said they didn't care about a tree, but I couldn't bear the thought of them waking up on Christmas morning without one. I hope you don't mind that I decorated it for you."

Barbara was on the verge of tears.

"Of course not! Thank you Santa's-helper-Sam! You helped make this a joyous Christmas for my family. It's so kind of you to think of us."

She stepped down to him through the threshold and pressed a warm kiss on his cold cheek. Sam blushed.

"I wish it could be more, Barbara," Sam said.

"It's more than enough, Mr. Adams—more than enough. Merry Christmas!"

Chapter Fifteen

December 4 – 11:30 p.m.

"Not bad, old man. It looks almost as good as new," Sam said, congratulating himself on his fine handiwork as he admired the little bike. He'd spent several hours that morning carefully polishing his grandson's old two-wheeler and as a result the bicycle practically gleamed under the dull basement light.

Sam stored the bike in the basement thinking that Chris would want to ride it when he visited. But by the time Roger was able to take a break from his new job and visit, Chris had outgrown the small bike.

As fortune would have it, the bike was red, just as Jason Wendell requested. A quick trip to the hardware store, earlier that day, for training wheels and a noisy horn had transformed the bike into a small boy's dream. A glance at the mantle clock told Sam that Christmas Eve was drawing to a close.

"I'd better get a move on it," he thought as he wheeled the bike out the front door. Lifting the bike with a grunt, Sam slowly descended his steps. Patting the pockets of his pants, Sam discovered that he didn't have his car keys.

"Ah well, it's just a short walk. I'll push the bike there and be home in no time at all," Sam told himself.

Sam stooped over and grasped the handle bar, ignoring the pain in his lower back. Negotiating the icy sidewalk patches was tricky to the point where Sam was tempted to return home and find his keys.

"Almost there, almost there," he intoned under his breath.

At last he arrived at Jason's house. A light glowing dimly from the window barely illuminated the front steps.

"What is it with steps?" Sam muttered. "Does every house in the State of Wisconsin have to have front steps?"

With a sigh Sam lifted the bike and heaved himself up the stairs. He leaned his shoulder against the screen door and gave a little push. Luckily the door was not locked and he was able to pull the bike onto the porch. Once inside, he engaged the bike's kickstand and set it just to the side of the door. He adjusted the big red bow tied to the handlebars and the tag that read, "To Jason, from Santa."

With Santa's helper Sam's final task complete, Sam was more than ready to head home. As he turned to leave, he heard a demanding voice from inside the house.

"Who are you? What are you doing here? I'll call the police! Do you hear me?"

"Pam, it's okay. It's just me, Sam Adams," he reassured.

The front door cracked open. Pam peered out, one eye showing.

"Mr. Adams? What are you doing dressed like that?"

"Why I'm Santa's-helper-Sam! I heard that you had a great little boy who wanted a big-boy bike for Christmas and I thought that I could help."

"Santa's helper?" Pam repeated as she looked at Sam and the bicycle with equal degrees of astonishment. "This bike is for Jason?"

"Well, unless you are partial to red two-wheelers with training wheels, I think that it's best that Jason have it," Sam chuckled.

"Mr. Adams, I don't know what to say. I don't have any money to give you for the bike."

"Nonsense," Sam reprimanded. "This is a Christmas present for your son, there will be no talk of money."

Pam hurled herself into Sam's arms and sobbed against his chest.

"Oh, Mr. Adams, this is the nicest thing anyone has ever done for us. You made Jason's Christmas wish come true! Since Charlie left, well, it's been so hard on Jason, and he wanted a bike so much. But, I couldn't get him one and I knew he would be so disappointed on Christmas morning, but there just wasn't any money. I've been trying so hard, but, oh Mr. Adams." Pam's watery words flowed together.

Sam wrapped his arms tightly around her and said, "Pam, you are doing a wonderful job raising Jason and we all can use a little help now and then.

"Go back inside before you catch cold," Sam said gently as he planted a fatherly kiss on the top of her head. "You better turn it. Jason will be up bright and early. Merry Christmas Pam."

She smiled.

"Merry Christmas, Mr. Adams—Merry Christmas Santa's helper Sam!"

On his way home Sam passed in front of his neighborhood church, Saint Ambrose. He saw two stray dogs playing amidst the lit manger scene out front. The pugnacious canines knocked over the baby Jesus in the manger and ran off. Sam saw this and stopped. He was tired. He contemplated. He walked through the fresh snow, directly to the manger. He picked up the Baby Jesus, wiped him clean and placed him back in the crib.

An approaching couple with their two young children, a girl and a boy, spotted Santa's-helper-Sam. The young girl excitedly pointed at him.

"Momma, Momma! Look! It's Santa Claus! He's tucking in the Baby Jesus!"

The family stopped and stared at Sam. Sam turned, noticed the huddling family watching him and placed a finger to his lips.

"Shhh! Merry Christmas!" he whispered.

Sam went to the back of the church and used the priest's entrance through the sacristy.

The room was dark but the door to the altar was open. Mass was in progress. Sam knelt in the shadows, removed his hat and beard and made the sign of the cross.

At the altar, Father Vince, wearing his green and red Christmas robe, was conducting mass. As he raised a gold chalice he noticed out of the corner of his right eye a kneeling Sam in his Santa suit. Father Vince placed the gleaming chalice on the altar before him. He turned slightly and acknowledged Sam with a look and a wink.

Sam smiled and bowed his head in prayer.

Father Vince continued his service.

Sam silently prayed, "Dear God, thank you for allowing me to remember the true meaning of Christmas—to do unto others…"

He paused.

"Thank you for Roger and his family. Bless them, keep them safe, and Lord, if it is your will, heal Kate's mom."

There was another pause.

"Thank you for the many meaningful friendships you've given me throughout my life. I have been fortunate."

He paused once more.

"And lastly, Irene, I know you can hear me; thank you, so much, for loving me like you did all those wonderful years. You lit my world so brightly, that I can still see what's most important, even today."

Sam looked up and wiped his glistening eyes with his musty sleeve. He made the sign of the cross, stood and genuflected as he exited the sacristy. As he left, the congregation began singing, "Alleleuia, Alleleuia…"

Chapter Sixteen

December 25 – 12:30 a.m.

Sam unlocked his front door and entered. With numb fingers he fumbled for the light switch. He squinted as light flooded the room.

"Mercy," he thought, rubbing his burning eyes. "I can't ever remember being this tired."

Sam looked longingly at the sofa, but he knew if he lay down he would fall asleep and wake up with a stiff neck. Plus, he needed to go upstairs and take off the Santa suit. He also had to feed Badger and he knew he should probably eat something since he'd been going all day with little in his stomach. He couldn't seem to remember when he'd last eaten. His body throbbed with exhaustion and his thoughts were on the fuzzy side, but he felt content. He hadn't felt this good about Christmas in years.

Suddenly the kitchen seemed miles away and the staircase looked like Mount Everest.

"I'll just sit for five minutes," Sam thought. "Then I'll get up and change and eat something and take care of all the rest…"

Sam lowered his tired body into the overstuffed chair. He sat for a moment, rubbing the hollow ache in his chest. The pain tingled in his arm now, but he ignored it.

"Just tired," he thought as his eyes fluttered. "Probably should get my medicine. I'll rest just a minute more, then I'll get up," he promised.

Sam's head dropped to his chest as he surrendered to exhaustion. He dreamed wonderful dreams of past Christmases, Christmases with Irene. The dreams were so real that he could smell cinnamon in the air, and taste the sweetness of her kiss. In his dreams they were young—so very young, and so happy.

The Christmases flipped in his mind like photographs on a nickelodeon machine. Vivid holiday images, like Irene laughing as she tried to stop a 2-

year old Roger from pulling ornaments off the tree; Irene with a mouthful of pins as she again patched the seat of his Santa trousers; the two of them embraced, kissing under the mistletoe.

In his dreams, Sam was so filled with happiness that he thought he would surely burst. Lucidly he thought, "This is where I want to stay." It was in his past—in that wonderful place full of joy and love, and without grief or sorrow, that he wanted to forever be.

A crunching, crackling noise accompanied by two thumps and a softly uttered curse interrupted Sam's reverie. Sam tried to block out the disturbance and return to the sweetness of his dreams, but they were already fading.

Sam struggled to open his eyes. The room was now dark, save from the glowing light of the fireplace.

"That's strange," Sam thought. "I don't remember building a fire or turning off the lights."

"Ah, that's much better," an oddly familiar voice said. "Hope you don't mind that I lit a fire. It was pretty darned cold out there tonight."

Sam gaped at the portly vision standing in front of the hearth. He shook his head to clear the cobwebs from his brain, but still the apparition remained.

"How are you doing old fellow?" the same voice asked. "You did another good job tonight."

"Who are you?" Sam demanded.

"Who am I?" the figure asked. "You know who I am, Sam. We've met many times before. I'm Santa Claus."

Sam looked at the man standing in front of him. The shadowy outline cleared and came into focus. Yes, the man was dressed like Santa, red velvet suit and all. And yes, the man looked like Santa with his curly white beard. And his voice—Sam knew he had heard it before...but when?

"Hey, wait a minute. You're part of my dream; that's it, of course. This is all a dream." Sam breathed a sigh of relief. That was it, he thought. This was no burglar dressed like Santa. This was all just a dream.

"Sam, Sam, Sam," Santa chuckled. "For someone who loves Christmas so much, you really are a tough sell."

Sam was put off.

"You expect me to believe that I am not dreaming, and that you really are Santa?" Sam asked incredulously.

"Sam, remember with your heart. We've met before, you know it."

"We have? When?" Sam demanded.

"How's Badger doing?" Santa inquired, abruptly changing the direction of their conversation.

"Badger? How do you…"

"Oh, and I see you still have my sack," Santa said as he picked up the velvet bag that rested by the chair. "Why, it looks as good as new."

Sam felt as if he'd been dropped on his head. "This is one heck of a dream," he thought. Badger jumped up next to him on the couch. Sam pulled him close for comfort.

"And Sam, did you know that Mr. Park treasured that tie holder until the day he died?"

"What is going on? Can this possibly be true? No…impossible! This is impossible!" Sam thought.

Santa watched as the emotions flickered across Sam's face. It was always this way. The initial doubt, followed by disbelief, and then finally…

"You really are SSSanta?" Sam stammered.

"Yes Sam, it really is me and it was really me all those other times. Times when you needed to believe and times when you needed help making others believe."

"I believed in Christmas, but I never really believed in you. I mean, maybe as a small child, but…"

"You always believed, Sam. That's what makes you so special. In your heart you always believed in me."

"But all these years, all the times I saw you, you always looked the same."

"Of course I'm the same! I'm Santa Claus, what did you expect?"

"Well, I don't know. I mean, it's been almost seventy years since the first time I saw you…"

"My, my, has it been that many years?" Santa asked. "Sometimes it's hard for me to keep track."

Sam was also having a difficult time keeping track. He was confused. He didn't know whether to pray that he was still asleep or hope that what he was experiencing was real.

"Mind if I sit down for a while, Sam?" Santa asked. "Christmas Eve seems to get longer and longer, what with the way the world's population is growing. Sometimes it feels like there aren't enough hours in one night, even for me."

Santa sat down in the easy chair next to Sam. With a slight grunt of pleasure he stretched his velvet clad legs toward the warm fire.

"Whew, am I ever tired. You know most people think that I never get tired, but let me tell you, this is one big job! I don't know how I would ever make it without all my helpers."

"You mean your elves?" Sam asked.

"My elves? Well, they really do most of their work the other 364 days of the year, getting ready for Christmas Eve and all. No, I'm talking about the Santa's helpers who help me out on Christmas Eve…helpers like you, Sam. They make sure the presents go to all the right people. They make sure that no one is forgotten. They help spread the true meaning of Christmas…to give lovingly and unselfishly to others."

"How come I've never heard of those helpers? The only helpers we ever hear about are your elves."

"Ho, ho, ho! The elves do help me get ready for Christmas, and they sure do love all the media attention!"

Sam laughed. Santa continued.

"But my other elves…er, helpers, they're just people like you, Sam. They help because they love what Christmas brings to so many on Earth. In fact, that's really the reason why I'm here."

"What do you mean?"

"Like I said, Sam, this world keeps growing and that means my job just keeps getting bigger. I sure could use some more help, and I think that you would be perfect for the job I have in mind."

Sam swallowed hard. He gripped Badger tightly. Santa elaborated.

"I want you come with me and be one of my full-time helpers." Santa paused. "*It's time*, Sam."

"You're asking me to go with you and be your helper?"

"Now Sam, I don't have to convince you how important Christmas is, do I?"

"Well, no…"

"And I don't have to remind you that there are millions who need the love and joy of the Christmas spirit of giving in their lives…right?"

"Right. It's just that…" A scared Sam silently stared. "I don't understand. Do I help you for a week, a month, a year? What are you asking me to do?"

"Sam, I want you to come and help me *forever*."

Sam shook his head. He was still uncertain.

"It's time, Sam."

"Tonight?"

"Yes, Sam, tonight."

"Shouldn't I pack some things?"

"No Sam. You don't need to take anything with you."

"But what about Badger? Can I bring Badger with me?"

"Sorry Sam. It isn't time for Badger." Santa paused and continued. "I believe there was one person left on your list tonight. Did you forget?"

Sam cupped his chin and wondered whom he left out.

"Doug! Santa I forgot Doug! But what can I give him?" Sam asked.

Santa smiled at Sam and looked at Badger.

It registered for Sam.

"You don't mean?"

"It would make Doug very happy."

Sam petted his friend.

"I don't know, Santa. Badger's been with me for a long time."

"Trust me, Sam. Now is the right time for Doug to have Badger."

"Yes, yes, Badger does need someone to take better care of him."

Sam stood enthusiastically. He was no longer tired. He checked his watch. It was 5:30 a.m.

Sam looked down at Badger. "This is the right thing for both you and Doug. Santa's right."

Sam looked up and noticed that Santa was gone. No one was in the chair.

"Santa? Where are you?" There was no answer. A bewildered Sam pinched himself. There was no evidence of anyone being in the room. The once-hot fire was gone.

"What on earth?" Sam muttered. "I must be losing my mind. It was all a dream—just a dream after all."

A loud, impatient meow broke the silence. Knowing the tone, Sam glanced down and saw Badger looking up at him. He scooped up Badger and gently scratched the cat's ears. Badger snuggled comfortably into the white fur trim of Sam's Santa jacket.

"Yes, old fellow. It's time for you to have a new home, and I have just the right place for you. Some place where you will be safe, and loved, and where no one will forget to feed you."

Fearful that he might change his mind, Sam carried Badger into the kitchen, gathered his few cans of food, his brush and his dish and placed them inside a brown paper bag. With Badger tucked warmly in his coat he hurried out the back door.

The walk to Doug's house was about a quarter mile, but in Sam's view he got there much too quickly. Sam waddled down Dunbar whistling "Jingle Bells." He approached Doug's house and stood on the front porch under a still dark sky. Sam was sure Doug would soon be poking around under the tree to see what Santa left him. Taking a deep breath, Sam banged on the front door and hollered, "Ho, ho, ho!" in his loudest voice. He heard footsteps pounding down the hallway as someone ran to answer the door. The footsteps stopped and Sam knew that an eye was peering at him through the peephole.

"Yowee! It's Santa! It's Santa!"

Doug, wearing flannel pajamas and jumping wildly up and down, flung the door wide open.

"Santa, Santa, did you forget to bring me something? I've been real good all year. Yes I have…yes I have!"

"Well, Doug, I have one more present for you. It's one that I couldn't leave under the tree. I needed to give this one to you in person because there are some very special instructions that go with this present."

"Another present! Another present for me?" Doug hopped anxiously from one foot to the other. "What did you bring me Santa?"

Carefully Sam pulled Badger from inside his jacket.

"This Doug—I brought you your very own pet. His name is Badger and he is very, very special."

Doug's eyes lit up like a Fourth of July fireworks display.

"Oh, oh, oh, for me Santa! It's just what I wished for!"

"Here you go Doug," Sam said as he handed Badger to his new owner.

Doug ever so tenderly stroked the cat's head, crooning, "Badger, Badger, my new kitty cat. I love you! I love you! I will take very good care of you." Doug looked to Sam. "I knew you would bring me a pet, Santa. I just knew it! Just like you promised!"

Badger purred with delight as Doug gently hugged him.

"This bag has Badger's dish and a few cans of his favorite food," Sam said, opening the bag to show Doug its contents. "You can ask Barbara Donovan for help. She'll teach you how to take really good care of Badger. Do you understand, Doug?"

"Oh, yes Santa. I understand." Doug said, nodding. "Ask Barbara. She will help me. I will, I will," Doug promised, his head bobbing furiously.

"Merry Christmas Doug."

Doug cradled Badger in his arms and swung him gently to and fro.

"Merry Christmas Santa. Badger is the best Christmas present in the whole world! Thank you Santa! Merry Christmas Santa! Thank you! Thank you!"

Sam shook his head in wonderment and he walked down the steps. Giving Badger to Doug should have made him sad, but he felt just plain happy. He knew it was the right thing for Doug and for Badger and probably even for him.

Pink fingers reached across the pre-dawn eastern sky as Sam began his slow walk home. Lights twinkled from house to house. Children had been patient long enough and parents were finally giving in to their early morning enthusiasm.

Sam paused outside the Donovan house. There, in the front picture window, was a Christmas tree, *his* Christmas tree. The tree's lights gleamed brightly and the star on top shined with what seemed an inner light. He imagined Barbara's children's surprise when they saw the tree and it made him even happier.

Sam came to Jason Wendell's house. Stopping on the sidewalk he looked up at the two-family home with the enclosed front porch and smiled as he remembered how heavy the bike seemed the night before when he lugged it up the steps.

"I promise, Mommy, I promise!" Jason's voice broke the dawn silence.

"What is he promising?" Sam wondered.

"Just on the porch, young man," Jason's mom admonished.

"I know, I know. But I gotta practice so we can take the training wheels off!"

"Santa just brought you that bike and you need to practice with the training wheels first!" his mother insisted.

The front door opened and Jason eagerly rolled out his new bike. Once on the porch he hopped on like he was saddling a pony.

"Look at me Mommy! I can ride! I can ride!"

Sam continued walking. Jason's happiness reached out and touched Sam. It had been a good night. Sam was almost home when he glanced at Mrs. Cohen's house.

"Well, I'll be darned," he whispered.

A flickering light shone through the black metal bars and lace curtains on her front window, and in that faint glow Sam made out the image of Sadie sitting in front of her favorite chair watching television—*his* television.

"What a great night!" Sam thought as he made his way up his front walkway.

He hesitated and peered intently at his house. He could tell something was wrong. He was certain the house was dark when he left. Or was it?

Sam rubbed his eyes, trying to remember.

Warily he walked up the steps and slowly crossed the porch to the front door. Puzzled, he stared through the living room window at the bright light. A familiar voice startled him.

"Sam."

Sam turned around and got a glimpse of Santa standing on the porch. Thinking he was seeing things he blinked hard and Santa was no longer there. He turned and walked into the well-lit living room. A smiling Roger and his wife were seated and holding hands. They watched as their excited young kids in pajamas opened presents on the floor in front of the tree. Sam sat down on the edge of his chair. But, no one noticed him. Sam closed and rubbed his eyes.

Sam opened his eyes to find no one there—no Roger, Kate or the kids. The Christmas tree was gone. This clearly alarmed Sam.

"Is this another dream? I mean, this *better* be a dream!" Sam thought.

The familiar voice appeared once again.

"No, Sam. This isn't a dream. This is real," Santa said.

Sam groaned. He looked up and found his old friend standing before him.

"What is going on? Please tell me!" Sam pleaded.

"Sam, I told you. It's time for you to come with me. Not only could I really use your help, but Irene is waiting for you."

Sam became excited.

"Irene? Irene! Irene is at the North Pole?"

"Yes, Sam, but we have a long trip ahead of us so I'll have plenty of time to answer all of your questions…"

"You're sure this is not a dream?

"No, Sam, you're not dreaming. And yes, it's the end…on this plane… but the beginning on another. You've made a lot of people very happy over the years. There is nothing more for you to do…your work here is done. You've done an outstanding job, Sam."

Sam mulled over Santa's words. He hesitated as Santa walked through the threshold and began descending the steps. He turned to a petrified Sam.

"What's wrong, Sam? Is there something you don't understand?"

"No…it's just…I want to shut the lights off, okay?" Sam pensively replied.

Santa nodded.

Sam turned to the living room. He paused and glanced back to a watching Santa.

"It's okay, Sam. Go ahead." Santa motioned him ahead.

Sam stepped into the living room and scanned his many precious possessions—the keepsakes and mementos of a life well lived. He noticed the graduation, wedding and anniversary pictures on the mantle. He looked to the fireplace of smoldering ashes, and to his favorite sitting chair…and to his amazement, he saw *himself*—seated in his chair, his head slumped forward. His chin rested motionless on his chest. Sam stared at himself for several long seconds.

Sam now understood. He slowly backed out of the living room and started to walk out the front door where Santa stood.

However, Sam abruptly stopped. At the threshold he turned and again stared at his lifeless, seated figure. Boldly he walked back to his body. He removed from his coat the Popsicle snowflake and placed it on his empty lap. He turned, flicked off the light and shut the door behind him as he left.

"Now I'm ready Santa," he confidently said. "I can't wait to see Irene."

"Let's go then, Sam."

Sam and Santa walked away side-by-side down the neighborhood sidewalk. A gorgeous pink and yellow sunrise lit the beginning of their journey.

"How's Wisconsin gonna do next year in football, Sam?"

"Not too bad Santa, not bad at all…they've got this new quarterback…"

The sky bloomed a brilliant gold as Santa and Sam faded magically upward into the glowing light.

The End.

Epilogue

The modern American legend of Santa Claus is universally appealing. Outside the United States, the children of other countries faithfully anticipate the arrival of their annual, gift-bearing counterparts:

Saint Nikolaas from the Dutch…

Father Christmas from the English…

Kris Kringle from the Germans…

La Befana from the Italians…

Bobouschka (a grandmotherly figure) from the Russians…

Christkindl or "Christ Child" (girl angel) from the Swiss…

Pere Noel from the French, Brazilians, and Peruvians…

Julenisse from the Scandinavians…

Julemanden from Denmark…

Julesvenn from the Norse (Norway)…

Jultomen from the Swiss…

Hoteisosho or "Jizo" from the Japanese…

Joulupukki from the Finnish…

Nino Jesus from Costa Rica, Columbia and Mexico…

The Three Kings (Los Reyes Magos: Melchor, Gaspar and Baltasar) from Spain and Puerto Rico…

Kerstman from the Netherlands…

Shengdon Laoren "Christmas old man" from the Chinese…

In many countries around the world, regardless of race, color or creed, Santa remains the ageless, timeless, grandfatherly image who bears gifts that bring love, joy and happiness for all at Christmas.